CHRIST EMPOWERED
LIVING

DEDICATION

To John Muys in appreciation of his persistency in
encouraging me to share with a wider audience
the concepts I have taught over the years
to small groups of students.

CONTENTS

FOREWORD

Perhaps my fondest memory from growing up years is a scene repeated many times. I was raised in the north-eastern part of the United States where winters were cold.

On mornings when my bedroom window was frosted with ice, I would crawl out from under warm covers and, before anyone else was stirring, I would drag my blanket and pillow to a spot just off the kitchen and lie down on the cold tile floor. With head on pillow and blanket wrapped around me, with comic book in hand and a nearby lamp switched on, I positioned my unsocked feet just the right distance from the heater and let warm air blow through my toes.

Soon my bathrobed mother would appear, greet me with a curious smile, then go to work back and forth between the refrigerator and the stove. A hot breakfast reliably arrived within fifteen or twenty minutes. Dad, already in shirt and tie, walked down the hallway a few minutes before it was time to eat, stepped over me, looked down at me with the same curious smile, then sat in his chair and began reading his Bible, sipping the hot coffee placed before him.

All was right in my world. That's what I remember the most, the sense that all was right. My physical needs were amply met: good food I didn't prepare, warm air I didn't pay for, nice clothes I would soon put on and trot off to school. I was *comfortable*.

And my soul needs were also well provided for. A calmly busy mother working on my behalf, a father who anchored his sometimes difficult life in the Bible (I didn't know it was difficult till later), and an older brother who was never early for breakfast, who I fought with a lot but who was my fiercest advocate when anyone else took me on. I was *secure*.

Reciting this story is no mere exercise in nostalgia. It rather arouses my longing for what's ahead. One day I will be fully *comfortable* in my heavenly Father's house, responsible only to enjoy His limitless provisions. And I will be fully *secure*, gladly submissive to every whim of His infinitely loving heart, at home, fully at home, at last.

But where I live now isn't always comfortable or secure. Like you, I'm between homes. I didn't need counsel as the warm air blew over my feet and I certainly won't need it when I get to my eternal home. But, again like you, I need counsel now. I need wise understanding and clear direction to manoeuvre my way through cold winters where I must pay for the heat and through empty seasons where no one puts food in front of me. My soul is troubled, and it is hungry.

I need help to believe what I could more easily believe when I was a child, and I need wisdom to answer questions I never asked then. And I need hope, hope that is sunk deeply into the reality of what's true now and what's coming later. Sometimes the coldness gets into my heart and I can't see the reality of God, I can't feel the warmth of His love.

Selwyn Hughes is a longtime friend and a respected mentor ahead of me on the path. As I read the book you now hold, at many points I felt myself relaxing like I did so many years ago in front of the heater. At other points, I felt a confidence emerging that made me want to get dressed and brave whatever coldness might greet me on my way into the school of life where I stumble badly, feel confused and have so much to learn. At still other points I was quieted, not as a child is quieted, but more as a man who rests in a Presence that eclipses all other reality.

I have been a psychologist for more than thirty years. One thing I know. The field of counselling needs a wise voice to speak into our confusion, to lift us out of our narcissism and to direct us toward an encounter with Christ that has the power to actually change lives.

Selwyn speaks with that voice. I believe God has been preparing Selwyn for many years, through hardships and joys, through speaking and silence, to write this book. With its presentation of an insistently and consistently biblical and Christ-centred understanding of people, problems and solutions, and with its passionate desire to glorify God as transcendent in His purposes and to enjoy Him as immanent in His incarnation, Selwyn's latest work calls us from the memory of one home to the reality of a better one.

Selwyn is a sure and wise guide to all who live between two homes, to all who realise they are on a journey, a sometimes difficult one, to God. It is a joy to commend this book to a worldwide audience.

Dr Larry Crabb
New Way Ministries

PREFACE

A good deal of my life has been spent counselling people with problems. Most of them have been Christians, people whose character and standing were in no doubt. With this group I have been forced to conclude that the majority were definitely not hypocrites; they were good men and women. Yet they lacked the inner strength and poise which the New Testament says is the inevitable consequence of Christ living.

Endless hours have been spent trying to help such people understand and overcome those things that hinder the life of God within them spreading to all parts of their personalities. Often I found the cause of their problems was that they had not given Christ access to the whole of their being, and thus they were almost the same defeated people they were before they accepted Him into their lives. Knowing Christ had not made much difference in their lives.

This book contains the spiritual rationale by which I have operated in helping such people overcome their problems and move towards the kind of life where they exchange their own natural enthusiasm for Christ's abundant and inexhaustible resources – to experience *Christ Empowered Living*. I am convinced that the human soul can only be satisfied when Christ becomes the prime focus of its attention. Only He can assuage the ache for life and reality that throbs in every human heart.

In many ways this book is the culmination of my life's work. I write in the fiftieth year of my ministry, having spent a lifetime studying the genesis of human problems and working out scriptural answers to them. I have been helped in this task by many others – some personal friends, whose thoughts and ideas have aided me in building a framework for thinking about people from a biblical perspective. I have drawn heavily on their ideas in compiling this book.

My deepest appreciation goes out to men like John Wallace, principal of the college where I was trained for the ministry; Dr W. E. Sangster, a famous Methodist leader who taught me to preach; Dr E. Stanley Jones, the well-known author and one-time missionary to India, who inspired me to write; Dr Clyde Narramore, the well-known counsellor based in California, and psychologist Dr Dan Allender.

Chief among them all is Dr Larry Crabb, whose counselling insights have added richly to my work as a preacher, writer and counsellor and whom, as you will discover, I quote liberally throughout this volume.

My warmest thanks, too, goes to my one-time colleague Rev Trevor Partridge, who worked alongside me for more than twenty years and assisted me in integrating new insights into the many courses we taught together in different countries of the world.

My final tribute is to Dr G. Campbell Morgan, one-time pastor of Westminster Chapel, London, whose monumental work *The Crises of the Christ* gave me my first insights into the way God designed our personalities to work and function.

I have written for plain people and avoided as much as possible the jargon of counsellors. To be as simple and as practical as possible has been my aim.

Eight key issues form the thesis of this book. I introduce them to you now so that they can become helpful guideposts for you as you move from one chapter to another.

1. The life behind and within the universe is the life of a God who is good and who has our highest interests at heart.

2. Relationship is the essence of reality. Nothing in heaven or earth can be greater than this.

3. God designed us, after His own image, as relational beings. We are built to relate first to Him and then to others.

4. Sin has struck deep into human nature and distorted the divine image. No longer do we function as we were designed.

5. All spiritual/psychological problems have a relational component to them. We live dangerously when we fail to recognise this.

6. Only in Christ can we live the life that God intended for us. He is at work in us to restore the divine design.

7. Our problems can be resolved and overcome only when we decide to put Christ where He belongs – at the centre.

8. God's purpose in coming into our lives is that He might pass through it in blessing to others.

Christ Empowered Living has been designed mainly for individual reading, but the concepts it contains can also be taught in a group setting. Comprehending the biblical reasons problems develop and how, through Christ's empowerment, we overcome them, contributes greatly to richness of living and spiritual maturity.

The first five chapters lay down the theological foundation for my thinking as it relates to the divine design that has gone into the construction of our personalities. God paid us the highest compliment He could ever give us when He made us in His image.

Some readers may find the first five chapters which set out to explain what it means to be bearers of the divine image and how that image has been defaced and deformed, heavy going, and may prefer to skip those chapters and go to Chapter Six where we come to grips with the issue which experience shows intrigues so many: How Problems Develop.

One biblical text has guided my thinking through this entire volume. It first appeared in one of the most passionate prayers ever uttered by the great apostle Paul. It is my prayer, too, as I invite you to walk with me into the kind of living God planned for you from the very beginning:

> *Now to him who is able to do immeasurably more than all we ask or imagine, according to his power that is at work within us, to him be glory in the church and in Christ Jesus throughout all generations, for ever and ever! Amen. (Eph. 3:20–21)*

Chapter 1

MEET YOUR DESIGNER

Every Christian longs to live a divinely empowered life, a life that rises above circumstances and is not beaten or defeated by problems. This is precisely the kind of life that is offered to us in the New Testament. It tells us that we can have the life of Christ as our life. Those who commit their lives to the Saviour can say with the apostle Paul, "For me to live is Christ."

This means more than receiving Christ's help, as a flower receives the energy from the sun. It means receiving Christ Himself. He is not saving us from without but actually living within us – thinking, feeling, willing in the life of His obedient servants.

Why is it then that so many Christians say, "If Christ lives in me and I have the promise of divine empowerment, why do I get so overwhelmed with life's problems?" If I were to count the number of times I have been asked this or a similar question, I think it would run into thousands. As a first-hand observer of the Christian life for more than fifty years, time and time again I have talked to many people who wondered aloud why, with Christ resident in their lives, they couldn't overcome the crippling anxieties, fears, compulsive thoughts or obsessive and compulsive behaviours that sometimes beset them.

On one occasion a woman, well-known as a keynote speaker on the Christian women's conference circuit, put this question to me: "Why is it when I am at work in my kitchen and I pick up a sharp knife, I feel strangely compelled to cut myself with it?" She raised this question with me after reading that Princess Diana had confessed in an interview that at one low point in her life she practised self-mutilation.

Then there was the man who told me whenever he entered a department store with a large number of entrances and exits he would be seized with panic if he could not remember how to exit through the door by which he entered. The thought that he might return to the street through any other door set up such tremendous anxiety within him that sometimes it incapacitated him. Several times he required medical assistance before he could leave a store.

How can we explain such behaviour – especially in those who claim to have Christ living within them? To ask secular psychologists for an explanation of human behaviour is to come up with answers such as these:

- You are stuck somewhere on the hierarchy of needs.
- You are genetically wired towards aggression and anger.
- Raging hormones are the culprit.

- Instinctual psychic impulses conflict with the dictates of society.
- Your drives have been reinforced by rewarding stimuli.
- You are an Aries with Jupiter rising.
- You are an adult child of unhappy and traumatic experiences.
- You are compensating for perceived inferiority and seeking to acquire better self-esteem.
- You are demon possessed.
- You have no will power.
- You have that kind of temperament.
- What you are telling yourself – your self-talk – gets you into trouble.
- You are having an identity crisis.
- You do not know who you are, and thus you have little basis for self-worth.

Theories about human motivation and what makes people tick get quickly translated into counselling models. Solutions range from taking medication, physical exercise, reparenting, casting out demons, changing your self-talk, getting your needs met, avoiding decision-making when your stars are not properly aligned, getting in touch with your inner pain, and other popular advice.

I believe God has something to say about what lies behind human behaviour. When we want the real truth about why we do the things we do, He is the Consultant par excellence.

OUR THEOLOGY DETERMINES OUR PSYCHOLOGY

When I started out in Christian ministry, I intimated to one of my spiritual mentors that I wanted to explore as fully as possible the roots of human problems. This was his response: "Before you go down that track, keep in mind that a good psychology depends on a good theology. If you do not understand how God put us together, what went wrong and His plans for correcting our problems, then all you will succeed in doing is adding weakness to weakness – which, as you know, never makes strength."

Psychiatrist James Mallory, in his book *The Kink and I*, put it like this: "A person can never understand why he behaves the way he does nor the importance and implications of his behaviour until he understands who and what he is."

Well, *who* and *what* are we? How do we begin to get a handle on this important issue? Before we can understand who we are and why we do the things we do (psychology), we must first, I suggest, learn something about God (theology). So for a little while let's embark on a theological crash course in who God is and what He is like.

Before we try to learn anything about the nature and character of the Almighty, however, let's be clear about a couple of things. First, we would know nothing about God unless He had taken the initiative to make Himself known. In his book *Evangelical Truth*, John R.W. Stott put it like this:

Since God our Creator is infinite in his being, while we are finite creatures of time and space, it stands to reason that we cannot discover Him by our own researches or resources. He is altogether beyond us and all the altars in the world, like the one Paul stumbled across outside Athens would be inscribed TO AN UNKNOWN GOD! (Acts 17:23)

Second, though we may know something about God, we will never be able to know everything about Him. Thomas Watson, the Puritan preacher, said: "We can no more search out God's infinite perfections than a man on top of the highest mountain can reach out and catch a star." Evelyn Underhill adds: "If the reality of God were small enough to be grasped He would not be great enough to be adored." If God were not too big for our minds, He would be too small for our hearts.

It is one thing, however, to say God cannot be fully known and quite another to say that God cannot be known at all. I have always liked the story of the five-year-old girl who rushed up to her newly-born brother in his hospital room, leaned over him and said: "Quick, tell me, what is God like?" The little girl shrewdly figured that having overheard her parents say he had just come from heaven, he might have some inside information. She was bitterly disappointed when all the newborn infant did was to make a few gurgling sounds, roll his eyes and fall into a deep sleep. That young girl expressed in her own way the deepest hope of the deepest souls who have ever lived: What is God like?

God has made Himself known to us in different ways. One way is through nature. All around us in this wonderful world, we see evidences of His handiwork. Earth, sea and sky abound with illustrations of the fact that someone outside of ourselves – beneficent as well as powerful – is responsible for this beautiful creation. The clearest and most revealing inside information we have about Him, however, is contained in the Bible, the Holy Scriptures.

The Bible does not argue that there is a God. It simply proclaims it. Its paramount concern is not to persuade us that God is, but to tell us who God is. Scripture opens in Genesis 1:1 with the words: "In the beginning God created the heavens and the earth."

When the record was set down, humankind had a clear concept – the universe came into existence not of its own accord but by a supreme being, the Creator, whom the Bible describes simply as "God".

An article that appeared many years ago in *The Welsh Churchman* (a magazine that circulates mainly in the Principality of Wales), said this: "To find out what really happened when the earth was created inquirers spent weeks gathering information, checking it, rechecking it and feeding it into a computer. The great moment came. All was complete. Everybody gathered around. A key was pressed, the computer began to process the information and within seconds this message appeared on the screen: 'See Genesis 1:1.' "

Some people seem to think that reference to the creative activity of God is found nowhere else than in the Bible's first chapter, but the great fact is stated over and over again in Holy Scripture. It is, so to speak, woven inextricably into the very texture of both the Old and the New Testaments (see Deut. 4:32; Psa. 89:12, 47; 104:30; 139:13; Isa. 42:5; Eph. 3:9; 1 Tim. 4:4; Rev. 4:11).

The Bible says many other things about God apart from the fact that He is the Creator. It presents Him, for example, as Preserver and Sustainer: "O Lord, you preserve both man and beast" (Psa. 36:6). It shows Him also to be a Governor and a Ruler. "He rules for ever by his power" (Psa. 66:7). Again He is seen in its pages as a Judge: "Will not the Judge of all the earth do right?" (Gen. 18:25).

When Noah exited the ark, God made clear to him that He was the earth's Provider: "As long as the earth endures, seedtime and harvest, cold and heat, summer and winter, day and night will never cease" (Gen. 8:22). All life is from Him. As John Dow, a theologian from a past generation, put it: "We came from his hand, and we remain in his hand."

WHY A KNOWLEDGE OF GOD IS IMPORTANT

But why is it important to know who God is? And what He is like? Knowing about God ...

- reminds us we are dependent, not independent, beings
- enables us to walk through life knowing someone bigger than us is in charge
- gives meaning and significance to our place on the earth
- gives us a true focus for worship
- shapes our understanding of morality
- gives form and structure to our worldview

- gives hope when we are weak that we can lean on someone who is mightier and stronger than we
- dictates our philosophy
- is the ground on which everything stands!

There is, however, another significant reason we need to know who God is and what He is like – because we have been made in His image.

Here's how Scripture puts it: "When God created man, he made him in the likeness of God. He created them male and female and blessed them. And when they were created, he called them 'man'" (Gen. 5:1).

Because we are made in God's image, it follows that we will never fully understand ourselves, or how we are designed to function as human beings, until we know something of the Creator who made us. Think of it: we are made not in the image of angels or of other celestial beings. We are made in the image of God Himself.

Consider with me a little more about this great God in whose likeness we have been fashioned and formed. Whatever the nature of Deity, historic theology has always called attention to certain aspects of it. Theologians talk about communicable and incommunicable attributes. The incommunicable attributes are omnipotence, omniscience and omnipresence.

A word about each in turn.

Omnipotence means that God is all-powerful, that the Almighty can do anything and everything – within reason, of course. God cannot make an aged infant or a square circle, for example, or cause two and two to make five. And because the Creator is all-powerful, He can never be finally stopped in anything He undertakes. "Is anything too hard for me?" He asks rhetorically in Jeremiah 32:27. Obviously omnipotence applies to God alone.

Omniscience means that God is all-knowing. Nothing is hidden from his sight. Divine omniscience operates in two ways – extensively and intensively. God is aware of all that is going on in the world without: "For the eyes of the Lord range throughout the earth to strengthen those whose hearts are fully committed to him" (2 Chron. 16:9). Intensively He is aware of all that goes on within. "You have searched me and you know me," says the psalmist. "You perceive my thoughts from afar. ... Before a word is on my tongue you know it completely, O Lord" (Psa. 139:1–2, 4). This, too, is an attribute and a quality that belongs to God alone.

Omnipresence signifies that God's vast being fills the whole universe. In other words, He is everywhere present. "Where can I go from your Spirit? Where can I flee from your presence," asks the psalmist again in Psalm 139:7. "God is everywhere," wrote St Augustine, "and the whole of God is everywhere." One of my tutors in the theological college I attended used to put it like this: "God is a circle whose centre is everywhere and whose circumference is nowhere." Such is the mystery of this divine presence. This characteristic also belongs to God alone.

There are other characteristics and qualities in God, however, that He has shared with His human creation – moral qualities such as holiness, goodness, wisdom, truth and love. In addition to these are characteristics of God to which we must pay special attention as they, perhaps more than others, pull into clear focus the fact that God has communicated something of Himself to the men and women He created.

GOD IS A PERSONAL BEING WHO RELATES

Did it ever occur to you that the first thing revealed about God in the Bible is that He is a relational being? Look again at that majestic opening verse of the Bible: "In the beginning God created the heavens and the earth." The Hebrew word for *God* in that verse is *Elohim* – which is, in fact, a plural word. There is a hint in those opening words of Scripture that there is more than one divine person in the courts of heaven.

Again in Genesis 1:26 the inspired record says: "Then God said, 'Let us make man in our image, in our likeness.'" Here again, there is a suggestion of society in the Godhead. A book I have in my library written by a liberal theologian says: "To whom was God speaking when he said, 'Let us make man in our own image?' He was speaking here to the angels." This is nonsense, of course. The Almighty was addressing here the other members of the Trinity.

The word *Trinity* does not itself occur in the Bible. It dates from the time of Theophilus of Antioch, around AD 1270. Nevertheless, the roots of the term are deeply embedded in the Word of God. It is said that the doctrine of the Trinity is a New Testament concept, but the Old Testament is not without indications of it. In addition to the two texts I have referenced, consider the following:

> And the Lord God said, "The man has now become like one of us." (Gen. 3:22)

> "Holy, holy, holy is the Lord Almighty." (Isa. 6:3)

"Whom shall I send? And who will go for us?" (Isa. 6:8)

"The Lord bless you and keep you; the Lord make his face shine upon you and be gracious to you; the Lord turn his face towards you and give you peace." (Num. 6:24–26)

If texts such as these do not explicitly and unequivocally define the plurality of the persons in the Godhead, they appear to imply it.

One of the great truths the Israelities gleaned about God was that there is one living God for the whole world. One God for all. Only One! This was their watchword: "Hear, O Israel: The Lord our God, the Lord is one" (Deut. 6:4). And by implication all other "gods" are "fabled deities".

This concept that God is a relational being and that there is perfect society in the Godhead was brought home most forcibly to me many years ago in a paragraph I read in a small book entitled *The Everlasting God* by D. Broughton Knox:

> The Father loves the Son and gives Him everything. The Son always does that which pleases the Father! The Spirit takes of the things of the Son and shows them to us. He does not glorify Himself. We learn from the Trinity that relationship is the essence of reality and therefore the essence of our existence, and we also learn that the way this relationship should be expressed is by concern for others. Within the Trinity itself there is a concern by the persons of the Trinity for one another.

That statement brought about one of the greatest paradigm shifts in my thinking I have ever experienced. What impacted me, significantly, was this sentence: "We learn from the Trinity that relationship is the essence of reality." Until that moment I had always believed that truth was the essence of reality, but here was a reputable theologian saying that the basic nature of reality is not *truth* but relationships. The more I considered it, the more right it seemed. This insight changed my whole approach to God, to people and to the Bible.

Does this mean that truth is unimportant? No, because it is truth that brings us to reality. C.S. Lewis put it like this: "Truth is always about something, but reality is that about which truth is." Reality, when we find it, has to do with perfect relationships. Truth cannot be fully grasped in sentences; it can be fully comprehended only in relationships.

In *Understanding People*, Dr Larry Crabb says:

> If one believes that God exists as three persons who are distinct enough to actually relate to one another then it becomes clear somehow that the final nature of things is wrapped up in the idea of relationship. The essence of what it means to exist, the center of everything, the core of ontology, can no longer be thought of in individual terms. ... There is relationship within the very nature of God. God is a personal being who exists eternally in a relationship among persons. He is His own community.

Ultimate reality, therefore, is personal, not propositional. In heaven we will not be discussing truth or doctrine but relating in the way God relates – beautifully, perfectly, eternally. No arguments, no quarrels, no dissension. Whatever else the three Persons of the Trinity do, nothing can be more important than the fact that they maintain within and among themselves perfect, other-centred relationships. That, then, is the first aspect of God we must consider – God relates.

GOD IS A RATIONAL BEING WHO THINKS

The statement that God thinks may seem strange. Surely you might think, *that is obvious.* But some claim this is not a rationally based universe and that things happen by chance or by random. Scripture leaves us in no doubt that God thinks.

One has only to take a Bible concordance to see that the word *thought* or *thinking* is applied to God over and over again. Here are just a few of them, taken from just one book, the book of Psalms.

O Lord, what is man that you care for him, the son of man that you think of him? (Psa. 144:3)

Yet I am poor and needy; may the Lord think of me. (Psa. 40:17)

How precious to me are your thoughts, O God! (Psa. 139:17)

The Bible shows without any shadow of doubt that God is a rational God and gives us through nature and Scripture a double rational revelation. John Stott says in *Authentic Christianity*:

> All scientific research is based on the fact that the universe is an intelligible even meaningful system, that there is a fundamental correspondence between the mind of the investigator and the data being investigated, and that this correspondence is rationality. In consequence a scientist faced with an apparent irrationality, does not accept it as final ... He goes on struggling to find some rational way in which the facts can be related to each other. Without that passionate faith in the ultimate rationality of the world, science would falter, stagnate and die. ... It is therefore no accident that the pioneers of the scientific revolution were Christians. They believed that the rational God had stamped his rationality both upon the world and upon them.

I like, too, the pungent statement of C.S. Lewis, published in his *Christian Reflections*: "We are not reading rationality into a rational universe but responding to a rationality with which the universe has always been saturated."

One preacher tells of two women talking together while waiting in line at the check-out of a local supermarket. One turned to the other and said, "You look rather worried. Is anything the matter?"

"Yes," said the other woman, "I keep thinking about the world situation."

"Well," said the first lady, "you want to take things more philosophically and stop thinking."

It's rather a novel idea that the way to become more philosophical is to stop thinking. If that were the case, we would not have had the famous axiom:

> Wherever there is a thing, there must have been a preceding thought, and where there is a thought, there must have been a thinker.

Just look around at the room or place where you are sitting right now. Someone, perhaps long ago, had in mind that one day in the future someone would be sitting where you are sitting now. And if you are reading this sitting on a rock overlooking the sea or on the grass in a field, then the one who foresaw and provided that situation is the Creator Himself. It did not just happen. Someone thought it and made it happen. "Wherever there is a thought, there is a thinker."

Everyone is familiar with the famous saying attributed to Descartes: "I think therefore I am." Descartes was making the point that because he could think he knew his place in the universe. The science teacher in the school I attended used to tell a story that one day Descartes stepped into a pavement café in Paris and the waiter asked him, "Would you like coffee, sir?" Descartes hesitated for a moment and said, "I think not," and immediately disappeared!

Let the apostle Paul have the last word on this point: "Who has known the mind of the Lord? Or who has been his counsellor?" (Rom. 11:34).

That is the second characteristic of God on which we must focus – God thinks.

GOD IS AN EMOTIONAL BEING WHO FEELS

Another communicable characteristic of God is that he feels. Some theologians throughout history have argued strongly that God is not moved by emotions. The doctrine of the impassibility of God developed by early Christian apologists such as Justin Martyr sought to distinguish the God of the Bible from pagan gods whose passions led them into all sorts of scandalous and bizarre behaviour. It is not surprising that some early Christian writers responded to the myths of Zeus' rapes and arbitrary vengeance with an absolute statement of divine impassibility. But what they meant to emphasise was that God does not have mad, shameful passions like the gods of pagan mythology.

The great Jewish theologian Abraham Heschel put it this way:

> To the prophet, God does not reveal Himself in an abstract absoluteness but in a personal and intimate relation to the world. He does not simply command and expect obedience; He is also moved and affected by what happens in the world, and reacts accordingly. Events and human actions arouse in Him joy or sorrow,

pleasure or wrath ... man's deeps may move Him, affect Him, grieve Him, or on the other hand, gladden and please Him.

More than any other word pictures, God chooses children and lovers to describe His relationship with us as being intimate and personal. The Old Testament abounds with husband–bride imagery. God woos His people and dotes on them like a lover doting on His beloved. When they ignore Him, He feels spurned like a jilted lover.

Changing metaphors, the Bible also tells us that we are God's children. The closest we can come to thinking about God and His nature is by thinking about the people who mean most to us, our own child or lover. "If you then, though you are evil," said Jesus on one occasion, "know how to give good gifts to your children, how much more will your Father in heaven give the Holy Spirit to those who ask him!" (Luke 11:13). Is there any greater joy that can flow through a parent's heart than to give to their child something they know the child deeply longs for? Multiply that feeling a million times and you get some idea of how God feels when His children meet His conditions and He is able to give them the gift of His Holy Spirit.

Philip Yancey puts it like this:

Think of a doting parent with a video camera, coaxing his year old daughter to let go of the coffee room table and take three steps toward him. "Come on sweetie, you can do it. Just let go. Daddy's here.

Come on." Think of a love struck teenager with her phone permanently attached to her ear, reviewing every second of her day with a boy who is himself infatuated enough to be interested. Think of those two scenes and then imagine God on one end and you on the other.

The emotional life of the Deity is beyond our power to comprehend fully. How can we comprehend, for example, that the Lord hears the prayers of millions of saints every day, some who are in deep pain, yet He is able to sympathise with every one (Heb. 4:15). Some will be broken-hearted, disconsolate, weighed down, while others will be filled with joy. How can God weep with those who weep and rejoice with those who rejoice in such measure? And all this without taking a break to gather resources?

In *The Pleasures of God*, John Piper asks: "Who can comprehend that God continually burns with hot anger at the rebellion of the wicked and grieves over the unholy speech of His people (Eph. 4:29–30), yet takes pleasure in them daily (Psa. 149:4) and ceaselessly makes merry over the penitent prodigals who come home?"

Who can comprehend it indeed? But we believe it because He says so. If we could comprehend it, then we would be as God. God's infinite nature is impenetrable by human beings. Just as God's thoughts are beyond our full comprehension (Isa. 55:9), so are His emotions. But though we do not fully understand them, we know that He has them. That is the third of the divine characteristics – God feels.

GOD IS A VOLITIONAL BEING WHO CHOOSES

God pursues his purposes through clear choices. Theologians have a word to describe this aspect of God. It is the Greek word *telios*. It literally means "end point" and is used to reinforce the thought that God is a purposeful being who moves determinately through the universe.

Christians differ about the mode of creation, but all agree that God created the world, by an act of His will. Over and over again in the first chapter of Genesis, we read these words: "And God said ... " Whatever God said in those days of creation came to pass because it was an expression of His will. We know this is so, for in the book of Revelation the worshipping hosts cry: "You are worthy, our Lord and God, to receive glory and honour and power, for you created all things, and by your will they were created and have their being" (Rev. 4:11).

Note again the words "by your will they were created".

A host of scriptures could be brought together to show that God is a choosing being. Here are just a few:

But God chose the foolish things of the world to shame the wise; God chose the weak things of the world to shame the strong. (1 Cor. 1:27)

But we ought always to thank God for you, brothers loved by the Lord, because from the beginning God chose you to be saved through the sanctifying work of the Spirit and through belief in the truth. (2 Thess. 2:13)

"But you, O Israel, my servant, Jacob, whom I have chosen, you descendants of Abraham my friend." (Isa. 41:8)

"If you belonged to the world, it would love you as its own. As it is, you do not belong to the world, but I have chosen you out of the world. That is why the world hates you." (John 15:19)

He was chosen before the creation of the world, but was revealed in these last times for your sake. (1 Pet. 1:20)

When the apostle Paul was confronted by Christ on the Damascus road, he was told by the Saviour, "The God of our fathers has chosen you to know his will" (Acts 22:14).

His purpose, say the theologians, is free, sovereign and immutable: free in that He cannot be under the influence of anything or anyone outside Himself; sovereign inasmuch as God has the power and ability to carry out His purposes; and immutable in that there can be no change in His mind, for change would imply lack of wisdom in planning and/or lack of power in executing.

Any discussion of the will of God must also take into consideration the aspect of divine election that God chose us in Him before the foundation of the world (Eph. 1:4).

God chooses and His choices are made with the good of the universe in mind. "I have plans for you," He says, "and my plans are good" (see Jer. 29:11). This then is the fourth aspect of our Creator's communicable attributes – God chooses.

Let the last thought in this opening chapter be this: Although it is possible to know something about God through the study of His attributes, it is not possible to know God intimately until one experiences what the Bible calls "a new birth". During our Lord's time on this earth, He met with a leading religious scholar named Nicodemus. Though Nicodemus had great religious knowledge, he had not the slightest notion of what Jesus was talking about when our Lord said, "You must be born again" (John 3:7). He could not understand the curious expression and thought it meant some strange regression into the natal cave, an idea that we know is anatomically impossible. The learned religious leader needed to understand that knowledge about God is different from knowing God personally – a fact that can only be experienced as one opens one's heart to the Saviour. Without this, there can be no real knowledge of God or of spiritual things. The apostle Paul makes the same point powerfully in 1 Corinthians 2:14: "The man without the Spirit does not accept the things that come from the Spirit of God, for they are foolishness to him, and he cannot understand them, because they are spiritually discerned."

I once counselled a professor who taught at London University. He had four PhDs, including one in theology, as well as numerous other degrees; but as we talked about God, he asked me several times to repeat what I had said, offering this explanation, "I can grapple with many scientific theories, but understanding God is beyond me." How different were our conversations after he was converted and came into the experience which

Jesus called "the new birth". He understood and saw God differently because he knew God personally.

A theological education can present you with possibilities and probabilities, speculations and conjectures; only a personal encounter with God through His Son Jesus Christ can initiate you into a spiritual world where you pass from knowing about Him to knowing Him for who He is.

In this chapter we have said four pivotal things: God is a personal being who relates. God is a rational being who thinks. God is an emotional being who feels. God is a volitional being who chooses. That same design can be seen reflected in His human creation, for we are made in the divine image. To that awesome subject we turn next.

Chapter 2

THE DESIGNER'S LABEL

On July 23, 1969, Edwin R. Aldrin ("Buzz" to his family and friends) was returning to earth on the *Apollo 11* spacecraft from having set foot on the moon. In a broadcast he made during that historic flight, he read:

When I consider your heavens, the work of your fingers, the moon and the stars, which you have set in place, what is man that you are mindful of him, the son of man that you care for him? (Psa. 8:3–4)

No doubt that question will be asked as long as the human race continues. Significantly, the Bible poses that question, "What is man?" in two other contexts: "What is man that you make so much of him, that you give him so much attention" (Job 7:17), and "What is man, that he could be pure, or one born of woman, that he could be righteous?" (Job 15:14).

DIVERGENT VIEWS ON AN
IMPORTANT QUESTION

Well, what is man? Nowadays some seek to magnify man, to elevate him to a position higher than Scripture accords him. But others go in the opposite direction and look to detract from his scriptural importance and place in the universe. I came across this in a science textbook I found in my library:

> Man is a cosmic accident, a bubble which has blown up on the surface of some oozy primordial swamp and is designed to burst into oblivion.

It is popular in today's evolutionary-oriented climate to see human beings as nothing more than superior animals.

And many say that the origin of life is a mystery. Not so. There is Someone who can speak authoritatively about the origin of man, and that is the One who originated the species – the Creator Himself. Consider what the Almighty says about human origin taken from the pages of the Bible, God's eternal Word.

But before we do, consider this incident taken from a small book entitled *Life*, which is the story of a Scottish poet by the name of James Beattie. At the time of the incident, his son was about six years of age and the poet was eager to teach him a basic lesson about life. The father secretly went out into the garden of their home and traced in a plot of soil the letters of his son's name. A few hours later the boy went out into the garden and, seeing his name inscribed in the soil came running in to his father exclaiming: "Daddy! Daddy! Somebody has come into our garden and written my name in the soil."

"You must be mistaken," said his father, "nobody has come into the garden, let alone written your name." The boy insisted it was so, and taking his father by the hand said, "Come and see."

Standing beside the patch of soil that bore his name, the father said, "So it is, but nobody could have written it. It must have just happened by chance."

"No," said the little boy, "it hasn't happened by chance. Somebody has written my name there."

Then the father let him into the secret and told him about the plot behind the plot, which was that he wanted him to remember that there was a Somebody behind his existence. He didn't just happen; there was a Creator behind everything. It was a lesson the boy never forgot.

Nor should we forget that there is a Somebody behind our human creation, the Creator Himself. In passage after passage, the theme of our divine origin is told:

Is he not your Father, your Creator, who made you and formed you. (Deut. 32:6)

Your hands shaped me and made me. (Job 10:8)

Come, let us bow down in worship, let us kneel before the Lord our Maker. (Psa. 95:6)

Know that the Lord is God. It is he who made us. (Psa. 100:3)

"At the beginning the Creator 'made them male and female'." (Matt. 19:4)

"From one man he made every nation of men, that they should inhabit the whole earth; and he determined the times set for them and the exact places where they should live." (Acts 17:26)

HOW IT ALL BEGAN

Let's pick up the story from its very beginning, as recorded in the first chapters of the book of Genesis. We have two accounts of creation in Genesis, one in the first chapter and the other in the second. In Genesis 1, we have a general account of creation; then in chapter 2 it gets specific. Chapter 1 gives us a cosmic view. Genesis 2 repeats the story of creation but narrows the focus to human beings.

In both chapters we observe that God did not create the first human pair until after life support systems were all in place: air to breathe, soil in which plants could grow, water to drink and so on. First comes light, then water, then earth, then vegetation, then living creatures. Before man appeared, a whole ecosystem awaited his arrival. Once the earth was ready to receive its first human occupants,

God said, "Let us make man in our image, in our likeness, and let them rule over the fish of the sea and the birds of the air, over the livestock, over all the earth, and over all the creatures that move along the ground." (Gen. 1:26)

Then when everything was ready for human habitation,

So God created man in his own image, in the image of God he created him; male and female he created them. (Gen. 1:27)

A similar statement appears in Genesis 2:

The Lord God formed the man from the dust of the ground and breathed into his nostrils the breath of life, and man became a living being. (Gen. 2:7)

My interest here is not just to defend human creation but to define it. And in doing that we need to observe that when you open your Bible to the first chapter of Genesis you find the same words repeated again and again: "according to their kinds". The phrase is found in verses 11, 12, 21, and three times in verse 24. What does this mean? It means that when God created living things He made distinctly different species. The fowl of the air, the fish of the sea and the beasts of the field were all created according to their kind. This truth is reinforced in the New Testament:

All flesh is not the same: Men have one kind of flesh, animals have another, birds another and fish another. (1 Cor. 15:39)

Mankind and the animal creation have a different physical structure. "You just cannot ignore those distinctions," says Charles Swindoll, "and maintain a correct Biblical position on creation."

Another verse in 1 Corinthians 15 has often gripped me, verse 45:

"The first man Adam became a living being"; the last Adam, a life-giving spirit.

This is a tremendously important text, for it shows clearly that Adam was the first created being. No one came before him in this category. No fowl was like him. No fish or animal could respond to God's love or harness and use the earth's resources.

The pattern God followed when He made the first human pair was *"in our image"*. Mankind was unlike anything that had ever been created before. Nowhere do we read that God put His image in the beasts or any other part of creation. No other animal in creation could relate as God relates, think as God thinks, feel as God feels and choose as God chooses. Only human beings have the image of God written into their very constitution. What a privileged position Adam and Eve were given. Surely it is one of the most staggering truths in the whole of the Bible.

Scripture teaches that we are the direct creation of God, not the consequence of evolutionary forces. God took dust in His hands and as a result we bear the divine image. No other creatures of God are handmade. We are unique. It means we are superior to all other creatures. And no other creature was told to rule over anything.

In the early days of my conversion, before I became a theological student, I used to think that if you were to draw lines from a human being out into infinity, you would eventually come to a great big God with eyes and ears and arms and legs, but a million times bigger than any mortal. Then someone pointed out to me that God is a Spirit (John 4:24) and though the Bible talks about God having hands and feet and ears, this really is the Bible's way of explaining the Deity's human qualities and abilities. Some, of course, insist that references to God's fingers, hands, feet, ears, nose and eyes are to be taken literally, though not even the most extreme would, I imagine, say that God has feathers (Psa. 91:4)!

But what exactly does Scripture mean when it says we have been created in God's image? Debates on this question have raged throughout time, and the view I now present is unlikely to be the last word on the subject.

BEARERS OF THE DIVINE IMAGE

Seven passages in the Bible refer to mankind as being made in God's image or use the word *image*.

Then God said, "Let us make man in our image, in our likeness, and let them rule over the fish of the sea and the birds of the air, over the livestock, over all the earth, and over all the creatures that move along the ground." (Gen. 1:26)

When God created man, he made him in the likeness of God. He created them male and female and blessed them. And when they were created, he called them "man". (Gen. 5:1–2)

"Whoever sheds the blood of man, by man shall his blood be shed; for in the image of God has God made man." (Gen. 9:6)

A man ought not to cover his head, since he is the image and glory of God; but the woman is the glory of man. (1 Cor. 11:7)

The god of this age has blinded the minds of unbelievers, so that they cannot see the light of the gospel of the glory of Christ, who is the image of God. (2 Cor. 4:4)

Do not lie to each other, since you have taken off your old self with its practices and have put on the new self, which is being renewed in knowledge in the image of its Creator. (Col. 3:9–10)

The Son is the radiance of God's glory and the exact representation of his being, sustaining all things by his powerful word. (Heb. 1:3)

The root idea of the Hebrew word translated *image* is "shadow." Two different words are used in the New Testament, one *eikon* (meaning a "profile") and the other *kharakter*, meaning "an exact copy or engraving". In both Old and New Testaments the expression means "a definite resemblance", except in relation to Christ in Hebrews where the language is descriptive of Christ who is God.

One great British Bible teacher, G. Campbell Morgan, in *The Crises of the Christ*, said this about "the image of God":

Perhaps the simplest exposition of the thought would be gained by a contemplation of the shadow of a man cast upon some white background by the shining of a great light. What the shadow would be to the man, the man would be to God. Like and unlike suggesting an idea, but by no means explaining the mystery, impossible apart from the substance and yet infinitely less in essence than the substance. Man no more perfectly expresses all the facts concerning God, than does the shadow those concerning man. Nevertheless the shadow is the image of the man and indicates truth concerning him.

To put it in its simplest form, being made in God's image means that when the Almighty designed the first human pair, He saw something of Himself reflected in them. "God created us," said Philip Yancey, "so that when he looked upon us he would see reflected something of himself."

But just *how* are we like God? In what sense were we made to resemble and reflect the Deity? In the previous chapter I suggested that God is a being who relates, thinks, feels and chooses. Genesis 2 shows us that these same capacities were written into Adam and Eve at their creation. They could relate like God, think like God, feel like God and choose like God. They were limited, of course, in the expression of these abilities (only God is unlimited), but the possession of these four characteristics constitutes the essence of the divine image.

RELATIONAL BEINGS

Men and women have been so designed that they are capable of entering into a relationship with God and with one another. The very first person whom Adam related to after his creation was God. Among the first words God spoke to Adam were to tell him to take care of the garden and ...

"You are free to eat from any tree in the garden; but you must not eat from the tree of the knowledge of good and evil." (Gen. 2:16)

Adam was designed, however, to relate not only to God but also to someone like himself – a thinking, choosing, feeling being. The way God went about preparing Adam for his mate is fascinating. Here's a quick overview.

Over and over again in Genesis 1 we read these words, "And God saw that it was good." The phrase occurs six times – in verses 10, 12, 18, 21, 25, and 31. In verse 31, an additional word is added:

God saw all that he had made, and it was very good.

In Genesis 2, however, where more of the details are filled in, a different note is struck. God points out something that was *not* good.

The Lord God said, "It is not good for the man to be alone. I will make a helper suitable for him." (Gen. 2:18)

Despite the fact that Adam was surrounded by the most wonderful creation – birds singing, deer gambolling, rivers rushing – he was alone. Not lonely, but alone. If in those days prior to the creation of Eve, God had asked Adam, "Are you lonely?" I don't believe he would have understood the question.

A clearer understanding of what I mean can be gained by considering a passage from C.S. Lewis's novel *Perelandra*. The story's protagonist, Ransom, is sent to the planet Venus to hinder Satan's attempts to seduce the planet's first woman, Tinidril. He encounters her still in her innocence on the floating islands Lewis tells us cover the planet. He puts to her this question, Are you happy? She is unable to understand the question simply because she had never experienced the opposite, unhappiness.

I believe it was the same with Adam. Enjoying God and the pleasures of a bountiful creation, he must have felt fully satisfied with his lot. He seemed perfectly secure in his singleness. We never read of him making any complaint that he was lonely. But in order for God's image to be fully revealed in him as a relational being, he needed someone like himself to whom he could relate – someone with skin on! God has designed us to relate not only on a level with Him but also on a level with other human beings. Thus, having only God, Adam was alone.

Note now how God went about remedying this situation. First, He brought all the animals before Adam in order that he might name them. The book of Genesis says:

Now the Lord God had formed out of the ground all the beasts of the field and all the birds of the air. He brought them to the man to see what he would name them; and whatever the man called each living creature, that was its name. (Gen. 2:19)

What was God's purpose in bringing all the animals before Adam in order that he might name them? I can think of at least two reasons. One was to bring the animals under Adam's rule. (When we name something, we bring it under our authority.) The second was to develop in his heart the idea that he needed to relate not only to the animals but also to someone comparable to himself.

After Adam had named all the animals, it would have occurred to him that for every animal in creation there was a mate. Was it at that moment, I wonder, that he began to realise something was missing in his relationships – that no matter how well he related to the animals, he was created for another type of relationship, a far superior one, with someone like himself? Cryptically the Bible says,

But for Adam no suitable helper was found. (Gen. 2:20)

How wonderfully and beautifully God prepared Adam for the encounter with Eve. Imagine if God had said: "Adam, go behind the bushes, and see what I have there for you," and surprised him in that way. He might have died of shock! Having caused the idea to surface in

Adam's mind that he needed someone like himself, with whom to relate, God then set about the task of creating a mate for him in this way:

> *So the Lord God caused the man to fall into a deep sleep; and while he was sleeping, he took one of the man's ribs and closed up the place with flesh. Then the Lord God made a woman from the rib he had taken out of the man, and he brought her to the man.* (Gen. 2:21–22)

The moment Eve was created and brought to Adam was the moment the image of God as a relational being was for the first time seen on the earth. Adam now had someone to whom he could relate on the same level as himself, someone he could speak to, see, and touch. The image of God as a relational being was complete.

THINKING BEINGS

Another essential feature of Adam's creation was his God-given ability to think. The first time we see Adam's thought processes at work is when he named the animals. Just what was going on in Adam's mind as he gave names to the assembled animal creation? His sinless and creative mind, I think, would have read the characteristics of each animal and named it appropriately. Take for example the word *hippopotamus*. The name means "river horse". Can you think of a better name for such an animal? It conjures up exactly what it looks like – a horse that spends most of its time in a river.

Adam's sinless mind, I believe, would have been insightful, so that he could understand the purpose for each animal in the whole of creation. It is my conviction that each animal is here for a purpose, to teach us something about life. Listen to how Job put it:

> "But ask the animals, and they will teach you, or the birds of the air, and they will tell you; or speak to the earth, and it will teach you, or let the fish of the sea inform you." (Job 12:7)

Bill Gothard in *Bible Characters* says:

> Adam's first task was to name each animal as God brought them to him. He could never have been able to give them precise names if he had not thoroughly understood their ways.

This is the first time we see man speaking, and to speak he must have used words. Thoughts are sentences we put together. How did he learn language? Did he speak the names out loud or just think them? We will never know. What we do know, however, is that thought processes were seen in operation as he focused on naming these animals and bringing them under his authority.

The second time we see Adam's thought processes at work was when, after meeting his mate for the first time, he says:

"This is now bone of my bones and flesh of my flesh; she shall be called 'woman', for she was taken out of man." (Gen. 2:23)

How did he realise that the woman who was now standing before him had come from a part of his flesh? Presumably because his mind was perfectly receptive to the divine Mind. God's thoughts, I imagine, mingled with his thoughts in a way that it was difficult to tell where one began and the other ended.

CHOOSING BEINGS

Yet another characteristic of the Deity we said was the ability to choose. We see this quality at work when Adam is given the choice by God to name the animals. Adam was no puppet or ventriloquist's dummy; the choice of what we would call the animals was to be his. Listen again to what the inspired record says:

He brought them to the man to see what he would name them; and whatever the man called each living creature, that was its name. (Gen. 2:19)

Note the words again: "*He* [God] brought them to the man to see what *he* [Adam] would name them." Here is Adam's volitional capacity being put to work. In effect God was saying, "All these animals are under your authority. Whatever you call them that will be their name. You choose." It was the same in relation to the woman. It was not God who named Eve, but Adam. He said, "She shall be called 'woman,' for she was taken out of man" (Gen. 2:23).

Another aspect of Adam's creation revealed his power to choose (and also Eve's) and can be seen in the words of Genesis 1:28:

> *"Be fruitful and increase in number; fill the earth and subdue it. Rule over the fish of the sea and the birds of the air and over every living creature that moves on the ground."*

Adam and Eve were given the prerogative of ruling over the earth, of being creative in it as God was Creator of it. Ruling meant action, not just reaction, and action implies choice.

Adam and Eve were placed in the midst of a wondrous creation. The environment in which they found themselves had not yet realised all the possibilities of its own being. It awaited the touch of Adam and Eve in co-operation with God for its realisation. Creation recognised Adam and Eve's leadership as it yielded to their dominion.

One more instance makes the point that Adam and Eve were choosing beings. In Genesis 2:16–17 we read:

> *And the Lord God commanded the man, "You are free to eat from any tree in the garden; but you must not eat from the tree of the knowledge of good and evil, for when you eat of it you will surely die."*

Clearly Adam was placed in circumstances of probation. In the garden of his activity, God marked the limit of his possibility by two sacramental symbols. Both were trees. One was the tree of life, of which he was commanded to eat. The other was the tree of the knowledge of good and evil, of which he was commanded not to eat. Between these lay an endless variety of trees and fruit, which he might eat or not eat as he pleased.

Of the tree of life, he must eat, and thus he was reminded in a positive symbol of his dependence on God for the sustenance of his being. Of the tree of the knowledge of good and evil, he was forbidden to eat, and thus he was reminded of the limitations of his freedom. Finite will is to be tested and it will stand or fall as it submits to or rebels against the infinite will of the infinite God.

He could eat of any of the trees and live; if he ate of the tree of knowledge of good and evil, he would die. It was for him to choose whether he would accept those limitations. It was a terrible and awful alternative. He could abide and rise or choose against God and fall into ruin. Yet, unless it were offered to him, this most important aspect of his nature – his will – would be atrophied, for will power having no choice ceases to be will power.

EMOTIONAL BEINGS

How did Adam feel when Eve appeared on the scene? Remember the last thing he had seen when he fell asleep was animals. Then, when he awoke, he burst into a love poem. Can anything be more feeling than a poem? Granted, the words in English do not read like a poem. Here they are again:

The man said, "This is now bone of my bones and flesh of my flesh; she shall be called 'woman', for she was taken out of man." (Gen. 2:23)

Hebrew poetry is difficult to translate into English. English poetry, generally speaking, has rhyme; Hebrew poetry has rhythm. Before I give you what I think is a good paraphrase of what Adam said when he first saw Eve, let me remind you of the last thing Adam did before he was put to sleep under the hand of God. He named the animals. Remember the phrase: "But for Adam no suitable helper was found."

It seems sad to me when people relate better to animals than to human beings. We are meant to care for the animals, but the relationship between human beings is meant to be on a much higher and different level. I accept the fact that some who are deprived of loving human relationships find joy in the companionship of an animal such as a dog, a cat or a horse, but there is something in every human heart that longs for a deeper relationship than any animal can give.

The last thing Adam related to before he fell asleep, we said, was animals. The first thing he saw when he awoke was someone like himself, the same yet different. What emotion must have surged through him when he awakened and saw before him the figure of Eve. With that in mind consider now the following paraphrase of Genesis 2:23, which is not original with me but borrowed from a friend:

> And Adam said: This is fantastic! I have longed for someone like this ever since I realized all the animals had mates, but there was no one just like me. This relationship looks as if it is going to beat anything I could know with the rest of creation. She will be called Woman because she was taken out of me, but now is alongside me. Wow!

Trust me, the Hebrew rendering of Genesis 2:23 conveys the idea of immense joy swelling up in Adam's heart. Like God, he was an emotional being.

Thus the picture we have of Adam and Eve in the garden is of two people created in the image of God, living in dependency and union with God, co-operating in activity with God. They were sovereign yet under sovereignty, independent yet dependent.

- Like God they could relate.
- Like God they could think.
- Like God they could choose.
- Like God they could feel.

Without doubt Adam and Eve lived in a perfect world. No sin, no disturbance of spirit, no suffering, no shame. The Almighty declared it "very good". But not for long. Not for long.

Chapter 3

WHO BROKE THE MIRROR?

When we look at how beautiful it all seemed to be in that pristine environment in the Garden of Eden, how free from problems of any kind, the question raises itself almost to cosmic proportions: How could something so beautiful go so wrong?

It requires little insight to conclude that something is wrong with human nature.

In *Understanding People*, the psychologist Larry Crabb says:

> The human machine has got its wires crossed somewhere. Some people get depressed when a friend is unkind to them, others seem happily oblivious to rejection. Most marriages begin with the warm of anticipated intimacy. Nearly one half of them end in divorce. Churches that begin with

enthusiastic pledges of unity sometimes divide into two camps, resulting in either cold war, hot war or a split.

To answer the question why something so glorious went wrong, we must turn once more to the Genesis narrative and consider in detail how God's image in humankind became fragmented and defaced, how the mirror in which God saw Himself reflected got broken. So take a closer look with me into that perfect world in which Adam and Eve lived, where peace reigned and beauty flourished.

In the garden, as we saw, there was only one prohibition. It had to do with one of the trees described as "the tree of the knowledge of good and evil". In a non-negotiable command God had labelled that tree off-limits. The Almighty said:

"But you must not eat from the tree of the knowledge of good and evil, for when you eat of it you will surely die." (Gen. 2:17)

Many people believe that the reference to the "tree" is a veiled way of talking about sex. The "eating of the fruit" they say, was really the act of sex, forbidden by God until the time when He wanted them to procreate. This is nonsense, of course. Something more basic than sex was at stake. The real issue was this: *Would they obey or disobey God's command?*

One preacher I know, David Pawson, describes the situation with which Adam and Eve were presented like this: "Imagine," he says, "you are sitting in a large library where no other members of the public are present. The librarian says to you: 'I have to go out for half an hour. You can look at every book you want to, but there is one book, right there on the top shelf, by itself, that you must not look at. If you do, you will be expelled from this library and never allowed to enter it again.' Once the librarian has gone, what would you do? Your action in either reaching for the book or not reaching for it determines whether you choose obedience to disobedience."

THE PROCESS OF TEMPTATION

In considering the biblical account of how it all went wrong, it will be helpful to our understanding if we note the process of temptation. The method was full of subtlety. This is how it is described in Genesis 3:1:

Now the serpent was more crafty than any of the wild animals the Lord God had made.

When the devil came to Eve, he did not come as a creature of ugliness but in the form of a serpent. He came disguised. There was nothing about him to be dreaded. A verse in the New Testament helps us get a clearer picture of his craftiness when it says that he can disguise himself as an ambassador of truth and goodness.

Satan himself masquerades as an angel of light. (2 Cor. 11:14)

When reading the account of the temptation in Genesis 3, we are watching a scene that took place before the Fall, before the serpent was cursed and consigned to crawling on its belly across the ground. The serpent was a beautiful creature, and there would be nothing about it that would have made Eve afraid.

But not only did Satan disguise his person; he also disguised his purpose. He did not sidle up to Eve and say, "I have come to tempt you and damn your soul." He never tried to talk her into becoming an atheist. He talked about God.

He said to the woman, "Did God really say, 'You must not eat from any tree in the garden'?" (Gen. 3:1)

What a perfect conversation opener – non-threatening and non-intimidating. There was nothing she could argue about in that statement. A paraphrase would read something like this: "Help me understand what God really said to you about eating of the trees of the garden. I just want to establish what God was trying to get across."

Eve replied:

"We may eat fruit from the trees in the garden, but God did say, 'You must not eat fruit from the tree that is in

the middle of the garden, and you must not touch it, or you will die.' " (vv.2–3)

From this we can clearly see that Adam had relayed to Eve the command that God had already given him earlier (Gen. 2:16).

Harold Robbins, in a sermon preached to a group of theological students that he calls "A Case Study in Temptation", makes an interesting point here in relation to Eve's statement: "God did say you must not eat from the fruit of the tree ... *and you must not touch it.*"

> God didn't say anything about touching it [the tree]. Some people defend God by becoming stricter than God. They not only know God's commands, but they believe they are holier if they go beyond those commands. There is destruction in that. Eve says, "You know we can't taste it, we can't even touch it." What Satan had done of course, was to focus her mind on that single tree, the one thing prohibited.

Let's focus for a few moments on the words "You will surely die." In the Hebrew it reads like this: "Dying, you shall die." I take that to mean the moment you eat of the fruit of that tree you will die spiritually and begin to die physically. That's the thought suggested in the words as they appear in the original language. The question is often asked: *If Adam and Eve had not eaten of the fruit of the tree of the knowledge of good and evil, would they have lived forever?* I believe so – as long as they had access to the tree of life.

The devil then sets about attacking God's word by suggesting that God was not speaking the truth when He told them they would die.

> "You will not surely die," the serpent said to the woman. "For God knows that when you eat of it your eyes will be opened, and you will be like God, knowing good and evil." (vv.4–5)

Martyn Lloyd-Jones said that the statement of the serpent, "You will not surely die", is "a dogmatic assertion based on a lie." I often wonder if, at the moment the devil said these words, he threw back his head, laughed uproariously, thus conveying by his body language this idea: "Oh come on now, surely you don't believe that anything like that will happen, do you – that you will surely die? All over a bit of fruit? That's an exaggeration. God said all that just to get your attention. Take it from me, nothing like that will happen to you. God might have said it, but he didn't mean it."

But there was more in this statement than just an attack on God's word; it was also an attack on God's character.

Look to the tempter's words once again:

> "For God knows that when you eat of it your eyes will be opened, and you will be like God, knowing good and evil." (v.5)

This amounts to nothing more than slander, a direct attack on God's goodness. He tried to impress upon Eve that God was not as considerate and loving as He appeared to be, or else He would not have limited her freedom. The implication behind His words was this: God wants to limit your freedom and stop you from reaching your full potential. He wants to keep you from the joy and pleasure that could be ahead of you. If you eat that fruit, you will become like Him, knowing good and evil, and you will have experiences that you never thought possible.

THE ROOT OF SIN

Oswald Chambers, one of my favourite authors, makes a deep and insightful comment in one of his books: "The root of sin is the suspicion that God is not good." Until I read that, I had always believed the root of sin was rebellion. Chambers, however, sees deep into Satan's strategy, and with a characteristic thrust of his rapier-like logic, goes right to the heart of the situation.

Satan understood better than Eve herself how her personality was constructed. He knew that once Eve entertained a doubt about God's goodness, that doubt would lead to disobedience. It is easier to disobey God when the mind entertains a doubt that He is good. I saw this statement quoted in a magazine some time ago: "When God looks bad, sin looks good."

When the woman saw that the fruit of the tree was good for food and pleasing to the eye, and also desirable for gaining wisdom, she took some and ate it. (v.6a)

G. Campbell Morgan described the process of temptation like this:

> Appealing to the intelligence of the woman, the enemy created an aspersion which was calculated to change the attitude of her emotion and so capture the final citadel, the will.

In these words Morgan gives us one of the most illuminating insights into the design of the personality that I have ever read. It throws a beam of light on how temptation proceeds and how the personality capitulates. Satan insinuates a doubt into Eve's mind concerning the goodness of God. Once that doubt is entertained, it soon affects the way she feels about God in her emotions. Then doubting God and disliking God (because of His limitations on her freedom), the next step is disobedience toward God.

This is how the personality functions: What we think greatly affects the way we feel and how we feel determines the way we act. Our will does not function in a vacuum; it is greatly influenced by what we think and how we feel. Doubting God leads to disliking God; disliking God leads to disobeying God.

Once Eve's *thinking* and *feelings* began to change, she looked upon the tree in a new way, through new eyes. She had listened to the lie of the tempter and then new desires began to take control. Her senses became alive to what was forbidden and the thing that was once out of bounds became something to be desired. Once God and His word were doubted and rejected, then quickly her senses became alive to evil. The next thing we read is,

She took [the fruit] and ate it. (v.6a)

But the matter did not end there.

She also gave some to her husband, who was with her, and he ate it. (v.6b)

FOR WANT OF A WORD

Note the words "*who was with her*". Adam, who had received the command from God not to eat of the fruit of the tree of the knowledge of good and evil, was actually there at Eve's side. Apparently, as the temptation proceeded, he said nothing. This simple but indicting phrase has largely been ignored by theologians and Bible teachers. But it shouldn't be.

It's astonishing how many people believe Eve took of the forbidden fruit, then went to find Adam so that he could partake too. The Hebrew text is quite clear. It means that Adam was standing at Eve's side when she was tempted.

Why didn't Adam speak up and remind Eve what God had said concerning the tree of the knowledge of good and evil: "You must not eat from the tree, for when you eat of it, you shall surely die." Here on earth we will never know. Scripture doesn't tell us why Adam remained silent, but my guess is he allowed his curiosity to overpower his reason. One thing, however, is clear: he failed God and his wife by not speaking in that crucial moment.

Dr Crabb believes that Adam's disobedience did not begin with his eating but with his silence. "It was a silent man," he says, "who eventually broke God's clear command." He says also that just as Adam failed God and his wife by his silence, the same failure is repeated again and again in marital relationships. A fuller quote on this subject comes from his book *The Silence of Adam*:

> Like every man, I am silent just like Adam was silent. Sometimes I stand dumbfounded in the face of my confusion. When my wife asks me to share even the smallest part of myself I occasionally bristle. When she cries I may become angry with her. Her tears frighten me because I don't know what to do with them. When she tells me I have done something wrong I defend myself to the bitter end. If she finds fault with me I find ten things wrong with her. I refuse to be wrong. I use words. I speak, but I use words to destroy relationship – as the serpent did in the garden.

Several years ago I spoke at a five-day conference of ministers in Moscow on the theme "The Theology and Psychology of Marriage". In that address I referred to Adam's silence and how it contributed to the downfall of the first human pair.

In the audience was a woman, a Russian poet, who was so intrigued by the idea of Adam's silence that overnight she wrote a poem entitled *For Want of a Word*. When through an interpreter she read it to me, I invited her to share it with the whole conference. Never will I forget the impact the poem made on that audience, particularly the last line. It hung in the air and for minutes no one moved as they caught the dramatic import of what was being said:

For want of a word Paradise was lost.

We would do well to ponder the words again: *She took the fruit and ate, and her husband who was with her.* This statement is the root of all our troubles.

G. Campbell Morgan described it most effectively when he said:

> The wisdom and love of God having been called into question Adam and Eve instead of taking counsel with him concerning the suggestion of evil acted independently and in that act of self separation from God fell from the sphere in which it was possible to realise all the infinite meaning of their being, into that of utter and irremedial ruin. All the rivers that have made sad the life of man had their source in this turning of the will from its proper channel, that of community of action with the will of God, into the channelless rush of undetermined and ungoverned activity. By the assertion of the will the first human pair dethroned God and enthroned themselves.

The Adam and Eve story continues:

Then the eyes of both of them were opened, and they realised that they were naked. (Gen. 3:7)

Up until that moment they had not been conscious of their nakedness. They lived in perfect and unpretentious innocence, enjoying the delights and intimacies of the relationship without concern for their nudity.

Theologians make the point that their nakedness was not only physical but mental and emotional as well. Just as there were no physical barriers between them, there were no mental and emotional barriers between them. They were at ease with each other and comfortable in every way. Immediately after they ate the fruit, however, they became self-conscious and were concerned as to how they appeared to each other.

THE BIRTH OF THE CLOTHING INDUSTRY

When Adam and Eve realised they were naked, they covered up.

So they sewed fig leaves together and made coverings for themselves. (Gen. 3:7)

"The most famous cover-up in history," says a preacher friend of mine, "was not Watergate, but the one that took place in the garden of Eden." But they hid not only from each other; they tried also to hide from God. "It was at this moment," said a quaint old North of England preacher, "that there took place the birth of the clothing industry."

Then the man and his wife heard the sound of the Lord God as he was walking in the garden in the cool of the day, and they hid from the Lord God among the trees of the garden. (v.8)

Isn't that interesting? Having partaken of the forbidden fruit and allowed sin to enter their lives, their whole behaviour changed. Whereas previously they ran to keep their daily appointment with God, now they run from Him. But though they ran from God, the Almighty sought them.

But the Lord God called to the man, "Where are you?" (v.9)

Here we come face-to-face with the first question of the Bible – "Where are you?" It is a question filled with much pain and pathos. The interrogative was really a rhetorical statement, because clearly God knew exactly where they were. What the Almighty was implying in that question was this: "Why are you hiding from me? You have never run away from me before. Why now? I made your hearts for intimacy with me, but you have given your hearts to another."

In their book *The Sacred Romance*, Brent Curtis and John Eldridge capture some of the pain that must have been in God's heart:

All of us have had poignant ecstasies of heart over a love affair that subsequently turned to immobilizing pain and shock as we realized that our lover could actually know us and yet leave us for another.

All this and more God endured in those terrible moments as He watched the first human pair turn away from Him.

I wonder how Adam must have felt as he replied:

"I heard you in the garden, and I was afraid because I was naked; so I hid." (v.10)

The man gave two reasons for his flight from the Almighty: "I was afraid", and "I was naked". How did fear arise in his personality? Two powerful forces drive the personality: fear and love. When love flows in, fear has no foothold. When fear flows in, love has no foothold. We are driven by either love or fear. "Perfect love," said the apostle John in the New Testament, "drives out fear" (1 John 4:18). Now that love no longer motivated their personalities, fear became the stronger driving force.

And what are we to make of the words, *I was naked*? That plea may seem strange to us today because we have never experienced true innocence. Children experience it to a certain degree, but it does not last long; once self-consciousness develops, there is a strong antipathy to being seen naked. From that day to this, it is a natural reaction with most people to cover themselves when they are naked.

Following hard on the heels of the first question comes a second: *Who told you that you were naked?* And before Adam had a chance to reply, the Almighty asked:

"Have you eaten from the tree from which I commanded you not to eat?" (v.11)

Have you ever thought about this? Why did God ask Adam a question when He knew the answer perfectly well? Had not the Almighty (who is omniscient, all-knowing) witnessed the scene when both Adam and Eve had eaten the forbidden fruit? Yes, of course, but the point of the question was to get Adam to own up to the act of disobedience. They could only deal with the problem after it had been exposed.

God's confrontation of Adam and Eve is one of the unforgettable dialogues in Scripture. Adam replies:

"The woman you put here with me – she gave me some fruit from the tree, and I ate it." (v.12)

Notice once again the evasion: Adam seems to imply that if God had not given him the woman, trouble would not have arisen. Instead of saying, "God, I'm sorry. I'm guilty as charged," Adam attempts to put the blame on the woman. A paraphrase would read like this: "God, the woman you gave me has caused all this trouble. I ate this because of what you did and what she did."

God doesn't argue with him but next confronts Eve, who must have been "shaking in her apron of leaves!" as Charles Swindoll puts it.

"What is this you have done?" The woman said, "The serpent deceived me, and I ate." (Gen. 3:13)

What a perfect picture this is of what psychologists describe as "projection", off-loading the blame onto another. As one wag put it, "Adam blamed his wife, his wife blamed the serpent, and the serpent didn't have a leg to stand on." They seemed to be capable of anything rather than face up to the fact that they were guilty as charged.

God then addressed the serpent:

So the Lord God said to the serpent, "Because you have done this, cursed are you above all the livestock and all the wild animals! You will crawl on your belly and you will eat dust all the days of your life. And I will put enmity between you and the woman, and between your offspring and hers; he will crush your head, and you will strike his heel." (vv.14–15)

Because of his role in the downfall of Adam and Eve, the serpent is judged and consigned to slithering across the ground. If we could have seen the beauty of the serpent, I think we would be able to understand better the judgment that fell upon him. How different the serpent in the garden must have been from the ones we know today.

God then proceeds to judge His first human creation in gender-specific ways. To the woman he said:

"I will greatly increase your pains in childbearing; with pain you will give birth to children. Your desire will be for your husband, and he will rule over you." (Gen. 3:16)

Presumably if Adam and Eve had not sinned, the woman would have brought forth children without pain. Now, however, she is told that birth will be painful. Also,

God said, "Your desire will be for your husband." What does this mean? It means that she would long for her husband to be the man God intended him to be, but she would be disappointed.

God's judgment on the man was this:

"Because you listened to your wife and ate from the tree about which I commanded you, 'You must not eat of it,' Cursed is the ground because of you; through painful toil you will eat of it all the days of your life. It will produce thorns and thistles for you, and you will eat the plants of the field. By the sweat of your brow you will eat your food until you return to the ground, since from it you were taken; for dust you are and to dust you will return." (vv.17–19)

The divine judgment was designed to bring them both to the place where they would realise, without God's help, they could not live their lives effectively. There would be resistance in their personal and public lives that would turn them back, time and time again, to throw themselves on the grace and mercy of God. The judgment was not so much retributive as remedial.

The Lord God made garments of skin for Adam and his wife and clothed them. (Gen. 3:21)

Robert Banks, in *God the Worker*, comments on the clothing of Adam and Eve by God:

This is one of the most anthropomorphically daring and theologically revealing statements about God in the whole of the Bible. It displays God's care for the man and woman alongside the punishment meted out to them. Although they have disrupted the delightful but delicate equilibrium of the garden in which God had set them and so no longer belong there but must face the threatening environment outside, God covers their shame more effectively than they were able to do themselves.

It was also, of course, a picture of God's providing for them a covering they could not adequately provide for themselves. It was a picture of the garments of righteousness that God one day would provide for all mankind through the innocent sufferings of His Son.

Theologians describe what we have been reading in Genesis 2 and 3 as "the Fall". Some people, of course, view the whole Adam and Eve story as a myth. Robert Louis Stevenson spoke of "the luminous Hebrew myth of the Fall". Is that what the story contained in Genesis 2 and 3 really is, a mere improving fable? Not if Scripture is to be believed.

DIGNITY VERSUS DEPRAVITY

The New Testament writers believed Adam and Eve to be real persons. So did Christ. Robert Blanchford said: "No Adam, no Fall; no Fall, no Saviour." "If there is no Fall," wrote H.G. Wells, "the historic fabric of Christianity collapses like a house of cards." He said also, "There is only one doctrine that can be empirically verified – the doctrine of original sin." The Fall is no myth; it is a grim and awful fact.

Strange though it may seem, however, the doctrine of the Fall is one of the most flattering to humankind. As Benjamin Fosse Westcott arrestingly put it:

> No view of the human state is so inexpressibly sad as that which leaves out the Fall. The existence of evil in so many forms, as self-will and suffering and vice and crime, cannot be gainsaid; and if this evil belongs to the essence of man as created then there can be no prospect of relief here or hereafter.

The Fall both flattens and flatters us, pointing at one and the same time to our depravity and our dignity. Blaise Pascal, the French mathematician and Christian philosopher, said: "What a chimera is man! What a contradiction! Judge of all things, feeble worm of the earth. Depository of truth; sink of uncertainty and error! The glory and scandal of the universe!"

Our dignity is that we are made in God's image; our depravity is that we carry in our personalities a fragmented version of that image. It was the tremendous dignity and worth of Adam and Eve that made their sin so terrible. As someone has put it, "A crack in an old tea-cup is no great matter, but a crack in a piece of the best china is a domestic disaster."

Ian Macpherson, another of my favourite authors, explains it like this in *The Faith Once Delivered*:

Suppose that I see a young man struggling along a street on crutches, pausing every now and again to "get his breath" as we say, and obviously proceeding with considerable pain. And suppose you come up to me and say: "That man is a world champion runner, an Olympic gold-medalist. He is the fastest man alive!" I burst out laughing. "You must be joking," I reply. "Why, that fellow can hardly drag one leg after another. Don't try to persuade me that he's an athlete." "Yes," you reply, "he certainly is. His present crippled condition is due to the fact he has recently sustained a bad fall, but he's a swift racer all the same."

To return to the question we asked at the beginning of this chapter: How could something so beautiful go so wrong? Here's the story once again – in a nutshell.

A tempter came into the Garden of Eden and, through temptation, succeeded in planting a doubt in Eve's mind concerning the goodness of God. That doubt soon led to dislike of God, and dislike of God led to disobedience towards God.

Having decided to live independently and rebel against God, Adam and Eve were cut off from union with Him. They passed into a sphere of living where their essential powers found no proper sphere of operation.

They once reflected so gloriously the divine image but now became broken lenses reflecting broken light. Now the knowledge of God is limited, the emotions degraded and the mind corrupted. Intelligence becomes bounded by its own limitation as it was severed from infinite knowledge. The emotions become dwarfed as to their capacity and tainted by sin. The will, a magnificent ruin, became perpetually attempting to secure mastership and yet will never succeed because it has lost its own spring of action – and its own Master.

There can be only one response from the Creator to all this:

He drove the man out. (Gen. 3:24)

The Fall was a relational, emotional, volitional and rational disaster. All grief and sadness can be traced back to that monumental day in the Garden of Eden. God made sure that Adam and Eve could not return to the garden by appointing an angel to bar their way.

Here's how Scripture tells it:

After he drove the man out, he placed on the east side of the Garden of Eden cherubim and a flaming sword flashing back and forth to guard the way to the tree of life. (Gen. 3:24)

By putting a bouncer on the east of Eden, God made clear that there was no way back into the garden. If there is a way back to God, then it must lie in another direction. But which?

Chapter 4

MAGNIFICENT RUINS

"The history of the human race," I once heard the famous preacher Martyn Lloyd-Jones say from his pulpit in Westminster Chapel, London, "can be summed up in four concise phrases: Man formed, man deformed, man informed, man transformed." We will look a little later at the last two of those aspects – man informed and transformed – but in this chapter I want to probe a little more deeply into how disruptive and invasive was the deformation that took place in the first human pair.

The essence of the Fall was independent action. Having doubted the fact that God loved them and then disliked Him for the limitations He had placed on them, they disobeyed and thus became distanced from Him. That inward and spiritual fall found its expression in the overt act of taking what was forbidden by God.

The words with which we ended the previous chapter are full of sadness:

He drove the man out. (Gen. 3:24)

Both Adam and Eve had by their own decision separated themselves from God. Having violated the command not to eat of the fruit of the tree of knowledge of good and evil, they were put outside the garden and its benefits.

But it must be noted that, though separated, they still retained the image of God in their personalities. The act of sin defaced the image and likeness of God in them but did not destroy it. They could still relate, think, feel and choose, but outside the garden they found themselves in a sphere where the essential powers of their being could find no fitting field of operation. They still had a capacity for God but no way of fully realising it.

Here's how G. Campbell Morgan put it:

As a bird cannot fly except in air and a fish cannot swim except in water, so man cannot exercise the necessary functions of his life save in relation to God.

Let's remind ourselves of the position of Adam and Eve in the garden prior to the Fall in order to see the contrast outside the garden. They were made in God's image as relational, rational, emotional and volitional beings and as such could be described as being the "shadow of God".

But not only were they created in the image of God; they were also made to live in a close relationship with God so that in their limitation they might find their complement in the life of the Creator. It is crucial to understand this point, for some have described the position of Adam and Eve in the garden as being on trial and given the opportunity of rising or falling according to the capacity of their own personality.

To quote G. Campbell Morgan again:

> It is to be remembered that they [the first human pair] were created in the image of God and then put in the probationary position through which they were to pass unharmed to some larger form of existence, if their life were lived in union with God. If however they chose a separate existence and cut themselves off from union, in that act, they would encompass their own ruin and would fall.

When Adam and Eve ceased to co-operate with God, they lost contact with God; and their powers of expression became dormant. Every part of their function as image bearers was affected – relationally, mentally, emotionally, volitionally and physically. The integration of their will, emotions, minds, bodies, and the way they related, was brought into disruption. They were "magnificent ruins". The Fall was a devastating thing.

Permit me now to pull into focus each of these areas to see how deep and pervasive was the damage that happened to Adam and Eve as a result of their original transgression.

RUINED BODIES

Take first the physical deterioration. God had promised that if they ate of the fruit of the tree of knowledge of good and evil they would die. As soon as they had eaten, the process of death went into operation. They did not die immediately, but immediately they began to die.

Physical death is the separation of the soul from the body, and spiritual death is the separation of the spirit from God. Henry Drummond, in his book *Natural Law in the Spiritual World*, defined death as "cessation of correspondence with environment". Death, therefore, should not be thought of only in terms of dissolution. The body dies and goes back to dust, but the spirit and soul are immortal.

But another thing God predicted they would experience as a result of their transgression was pain.

> *To the woman he said, "I will greatly increase your pains in childbearing; with pain you will give birth to children." (Gen. 3:16)*

And to the man he said:

> *"Cursed is the ground because of you; through painful toil you will eat of it all the days of your life." (Gen. 3:17)*

Let's reflect for a few moments on the importance and purpose of the physical in God's creation. The body was the spirit's probational dwelling place, that through which Adam and Eve received impressions from the world around and through it expressed the fact of their own being. A New Testament passage brings added insight to this thought when, in his letter to the Romans, the apostle Paul says,

Therefore, I urge you, brothers, in view of God's mercy, to offer your bodies as living sacrifices, holy and pleasing to God – this is your spiritual act of worship. (Rom. 12:1)

Herein lies a revelation of the true relation of the image of God in man to the rest of the body. Through the medium of the body, the truth concerning the image of God expresses itself. Where the body is presented, it is presented by the spirit; and through this devotion of body, the spirit expresses itself in worship.

In his epistle to the Corinthians, the same apostle expressed that truth this way:

Do you not know that your body is a temple of the Holy Spirit, who is in you, whom you have received from God? You are not your own; you were bought at a price. Therefore honour God with your body. (1 Cor. 6:19–20)

God-fearing and worshipping Jews believe that the spirit expresses itself in worship to God through the body. Jewish worship is intensely physical. I stood one day with some fellow Christians at the Wailing Wall in Jerusalem watching a group of Jews at prayer. I noticed the movement of their bodies as they prayed and asked our guide, a Jew, why they moved their bodies backwards and forwards. This was his reply: "When we worship God, we believe that all parts of our being must be engaged in prayer – our bodies as well as our spirit. The movement of our bodies is the outward expression of the movement going on inside us."

One of the questions I wrestled with as a Bible college student was this: Does the physical merely decorate the image of God, or does it define it? In other words, is the image of God merely in the spirit, or does that image extend to the physical also? Though I have thought about it for years, I have not yet come to a conclusion.

Some believe that even in bodily form, though in a secondary sense, humankind is a shadow of the Deity. As the body of man is the expression of his spirit and the spirit is the image of God, so through the tabernacle of man's spirit, certain suggestions are made of God Himself. Some theologians claim that just as human beings have a physical body, so does God – the material universe being His embodiment.

G. Campbell Morgan seems to have believed this:

> The essential facts of God's being govern all the forces of nature and so find expression in a thousand different ways through created things. What man's body is to his spirit all the created universe is to God. The Old Testament literature is full of this thought and so God is described as riding the wings of the wind, as making the clouds his chariot.

Christians will differ on this point of whether the physical universe is God's body, but among Bible believers there is no disagreement over the fact that as soon as Adam and Eve sinned there were direct and immediate physical consequences.

The body became the prison house of their spirit. It deadened the spirit's consciousness, silenced its voice, and the body became vulgarised. Though prior to the Fall there was perfect correspondence between the spirit and the body, after the Fall there was a discord between these two things.

Adam and Eve found that their disconnected spirits affected the physical and the process of death set in. Banned from the tree of life and with no way back to it, they were consigned to die. Of course, they lived for a long time after the expulsion from the Garden of Eden. Adam, we are told in Scripture, lived 930 years (Gen. 5:5). It took a while for the body to deteriorate until the seventy years we are now allocated. Clearly there were physical consequences to the Fall.

RUINED RELATIONSHIPS

Another immediate consequence of the Fall and into which we must look a little more deeply was the disruption of Adam and Eve's relationships not only with God but also with each other. God had foretold that this would be so.

Here are his words once again:

To the woman he said "... Your desire will be for your husband, and he will rule over you." (Gen. 3:16)

Many a commentator has puzzled over this verse, and some of the explanations I have heard seem to me to be quite ridiculous. But one of the best explanations I have read is that by Gilbert Bilezeikan:

> The woman's desire will be for her husband so as to perpetuate the intimacy they had prior to the Fall, but her nostalgia for the relationship of love and mutuality that existed between them before the Fall, when they both desired each other will not be reciprocated by her husband. Instead of meeting her desire he will seek to rule over her. In short the woman wants a mate and she gets a master. She wants a lover and gets a lord, she wants a husband and gets a hierarch.

How terrifying it must have been for Adam and Eve when their relationships became disrupted. You may wonder at my use of the word *terrifying*. But consider this: We are meant to find a quality of joy and pleasure in the company of others that is simply not available if we are alone. We therefore guard whatever threatens to move us towards isolation. Whatever threatens to separate us provokes deep fear.

And we fear those things with strong emotion. We were designed for unsullied relationships, and you can be sure that both Adam and Eve felt the loss of their perfect relationship in a powerful way. Eve would have wondered whether she could trust Adam since he blamed her for the problem when he said, "The woman you gave me caused me to eat." And Adam, too, would, no doubt, have reflected on the fact that had the woman not handed him the fruit and invited him to eat it, they wouldn't be in this mess now. Having to trust each other must have scared them.

Having been built with a desire for perfect relationships and now unable to experience them, they experienced a terror that was debilitating. Time and time again I have seen this terror surface in the lives of people in the counselling room when they share how their lives lack relational significance. In *Who We Are and How We Relate*, Larry Crabb tells of his encounter with this "terror" in one of his counselling sessions:

> A single woman aged twenty-eight had offended everyone in her community of friends. When at the urging of one particular friend she came to see me she knew her relationships were a mess. But she insisted with considerable force that the blame be divided between herself and the insensitivity of others. Ten minutes into our first session, she tilted her pretty head to one side, then arranged her mouth into a smile that looked more like a sneer and said, "I just want you to know that I don't trust you – and I don't really see why I should." I replied, "Trusting anyone would scare you to death." That comment after twenty more minutes of parrying opened her to talk tearfully about her most passionate fantasy – a wonderfully terrifying day dream in which she

trusted someone with good results. This woman was gripped by terror, a paralyzing fear that if she ever presented herself to people as the scared desperate person she was no one would be willing to bear the weight of her desires. She could be abandoned, left alone. And worse, if she offered kindness to another which she sometimes wanted to, it might be met with polite indifference.

Keep this thought in mind as you reflect on how Adam and Eve must have felt there in the garden. They were together but alone. They had lived together in perfect relationship – no fears, nothing concealed, no suspicions – each enjoying what the other had to give. Now they found themselves in an imperfect relationship that was beset by fear, suspicion and terror.

Adam and Eve, having showed themselves to be unsure of God, are now unsure of each other. They were made to connect with God and with each other in perfect harmony, each trusting and caring for the other, but now all that is missing. If we could have looked into their souls, we would have found a dread that no one would be there for them in the way their souls desired. What a sad and desperate condition!

Consider for a moment with me the dynamic structure on which their ability to relate was constructed. First, love for God: they loved God and God loved them. They could not love God in the same way that God loved them, but they loved Him with all of their being. In the revelation of His love to Adam and Eve, they responded in a limited degree to the love God had for them. A New Testament verse beautifully illuminates this thought:

We love because he first loved us. (1 John 4:19)

Adam and Eve's love for God was in response to His love for them. Seeing how much they were loved, Adam and Eve loved God back and in that loving relationship found fulfilment for their beings. "You ask me for a method of obtaining perfection," said Fletcher of Madeley, John Wesley's designated successor, "I know of love, and love only."

Knowing that they were loved and loved completely, Adam and Eve then gave to each other the same degree of love that God poured out to them. The love that God had begotten in them, by the vision and experience of His love for them, widened in their hearts to embrace each other. It was non-manipulative love, just like the love they had received. They related perfectly to each other and to God.

Once they doubted the divine love, however, and took of the forbidden fruit, the doubt they had of God's love began to show itself in their relationship to each other. They remained alive with a desire and a capacity for love but were left disconnected from God and from each other. They were unsure of each other, insecure in their relationship with God and also with each other.

This would also have affected the love that they had for themselves – self-love. I use the word *self-love* as opposed to the phrase *love of self*. Self-love is healthy – a healthy regard and respect for one's individuality and giftedness.

Love of self is narcissistic – an undue and unhealthy preoccupation with one's own being. (The difference between self-love and love of self is expanded in Chapter 14.)

If it is true that a fundamental terror lies beneath all our relational problems, the root of that terror is the fear that no one might relate to us in the way our hearts desire, then it is easy to understand how Adam and Eve sought to insulate themselves from that terror by building walls of denial and superficiality.

But not only was there terror in their hearts, there was also a determination not to trust. Probably nothing fuels determination like terror. They were determined to hold on to themselves and make their lives work without having to depend on God.

Their determination to look after themselves can be seen in the way they covered themselves following their discovery that they were naked. Their deeply-felt passion seemed to be their only chance of survival. Instead of turning to God and confessing that they had sinned, they arranged for their own survival by trusting in their own human resources. The root sinfulness behind that determination was their ongoing suspicion that God was not good enough to be trusted with their lives.

Adam and Eve after the Fall were not only fearful but also deeply determined people, determined to survive and fuelled by the suspicion that there was no relief from God or each other to cope with the terror of disrupted relationships. The Fall was not only a physical disaster, it was also a relational disaster.

RUINED MINDS

Consider now how Adam's and Eve's minds were affected by the Fall. Whereas before they had a clear understanding of God, now their minds were darkened. They could still think but not clearly and correctly.

Prior to the Fall, Adam and Eve were able to think accurately about everything. They understood the things of God – His purpose in creating them, their ability to be mini-creators, and the perpetuation of the glory of God through the human race. They chose acts that were in harmony with the divine will. Enlightened intelligence kindled perfect emotions. Seeing God clearly, they loved Him intensely and served Him wholly.

Recall the process of temptation. When one doubts God, the whole personality capitulates. It is a termite that brings down the house like a pack of cards. Adam and Eve entertained doubt about God's goodness. Doubt led to disliking God and ultimately to disobedience.

The truth once again is brought out in the New Testament when it talks about redemption being the restoration to mankind of the knowledge of God, part of that knowledge being the perception that God is good. The writings of the apostle Paul show that he perpetually recognised this fact as one of the most glorious results of Christ's sacrifice on the cross: mankind's restoration of the knowledge of God.

When writing to the churches, especially the prison epistles, Paul thanked God for their faith, for their hope, for their love and laboured for them in prayer that they might come to the full knowledge of God.

Here are some of his inspired statements:

And we pray this in order that you may live a life worthy of the Lord and may please him in every way: bearing fruit in every good work, growing in the knowledge of God. (Col. 1:10)

... until we all reach unity in the faith and in the knowledge of the Son of God and become mature, attaining to the whole measure of the fulness of Christ. (Eph. 4:13)

... and have put on the new self, which is being renewed in knowledge in the image of its Creator. (Col. 3:10)

The apostle Peter bears down on this truth also:

Grace and peace be yours in abundance through the knowledge of God and of Jesus our Lord. (2 Pet. 1:2)

Once Adam and Eve found themselves distanced from God, they developed strategies in their minds for bolstering their confidence that their lives could work without God. One of those strategies was blaming others for their own failure.

We have already seen how this works when Adam blamed his wife and his wife blamed the serpent. Blame is often a way the soul protects itself against terror. In the context of feeling terror, a terror fuelled by the determination to survive without having to depend on

God, their beliefs would have solidified. One wonders how long they endured with that doubt of God and doubt of each other in their hearts.

Clearly the Fall was a rational disaster also.

RUINED EMOTIONS

Look with me further at Adam and Eve's emotional spectrum and the impact the Fall had on their feelings. One of the questions people often ask in counselling sessions is this: How precisely do emotions arise within the personality? God designed Adam and Eve as reactive beings. He gave them the ability to think and their thinking, in turn, produced certain emotions within them.

When they were in fellowship with God, then you can be sure they felt only positive and pleasant emotions, like happiness, joy, peace and security. They fulfilled the command given later by God to all people:

Love the Lord your God with all your heart and with all your soul and with all your strength. (Deut. 6:5)

Every one of the emotions felt by Adam and Eve prior to their sin in the Garden of Eden was in harmony with that command. They loved God and they loved each other. Once they sinned, however, their emotions reflected the operation of sin in their minds.

Their minds – containing thoughts of distrust and suspicion towards God – soon affected the way they felt about Him. And once they had rebelled, they experienced emotions they had never felt before.

Three of those emotions can easily be identified in the biblical story of the Garden of Eden. First came guilt and shame. This can be seen in their attempts to cover up their nakedness with leaves from the trees of the garden. Guilt is an emotion that we attempt to compensate for in some way. God did not build into us shock absorbers to cope with guilt and then go about attempting to deal with it ourselves.

Bill Gothard defines *guilt* as God's way of showing us that we have violated one or more of His principles. The guilt that arose in Adam and Eve's hearts would have overwhelmed them. Here again, instead of coming to God and asking for His forgiveness (I wonder if that idea ever occurred to them?), they proceeded to engage in self-atonement – seeking to cover up their guilt by self-manufactured means.

Other emotions they would have felt are fear and anxiety. Adam, in fact, admitted to this when he answered God's question "Where are you?"

> *He answered, "I heard you in the garden, and I was afraid because I was naked; so I hid."* (Gen. 3:9–10)

They also feared that God would come down heavily in judgment upon them. Their anxiety would have increased as they wondered whether they were now facing death, as God had predicted.

A third stream of emotions was that of anger and resentment. These emotions can be recognised in the way they shifted blame to each other. We often displace our anger onto others. Feeling angry is not comfortable, so we like to spread it around and dump it on others as much as we can.

These three streams of emotions are still the main culprits in the human heart to this very day. Underlying all negative emotions is self-centredness and self-interest. Emotions that show love are emotions that are more other-centred than self-centred.

All negative emotions arise because of the absence of love. Where love is not, other emotions flow through the personality. One of the reasons we call them negative emotions is because they militate against the design of the personality. They are all anti-love. Where love is, fear is not. Where love is, anger is not. Where love is, guilt is not.

Adam and Eve's emotional make-up was at one time like God's, but after the Fall it became unlike God. Once they were separated from God and became unlike God, their emotions, lacking the driving force of true love, became selfish.

God loves in the very necessity of His being and in such a way as forever to make impossible the thought of selfishness. The deepest emotion of man acts finally along the line that will tend to the gratification of desires. We love those who love us. It can rise to high levels, but basically it is selfish and shot through with self-centred interests.

God's love is spiritual, self-sacrificing and is set upon objects utterly unworthy of His love, those who have given Him no reason to love them. Thus the emotions of Adam and Eve were depraved. The love they had was not love for each other, but self-love had turned to love of self. How different this was from the love of God that had shaped their personalities prior to the Fall.

The Fall was also an emotional disaster.

RUINED CHOICES

Just as the effects of the Fall were seen in Adam and Eve's bodies, relationships, thinking and emotions, so they could be seen in the way their will functioned.

The will desires mastery. Strong-willed people want their own way. They want the wills of others to bend to them. They get their kicks from this. This can lead to tyranny. God's will looks to others' well-being, not to mastering them.

The doctrine of the freedom of the will is itself true only within certain limitations. There is a sense in which the very nature of the will cannot be free. Only in lack of reason or madness is there perfect freedom of the will. Man never wills save under the impulse of a conviction. Behind every action of the will there must be a governing principle.

Humankind constantly asserts, "I will." The full statement, however, must always be, "I will because ..." That which follows the "because" is the authority behind the will, the power that commands it.

Although we will *because* of some reason that may or may not be apparent, the same is not true of God. Tucked away in the book of Deuteronomy is a wonderful passage that shows that there is no reason (as we understand it) behind God's love. God doesn't need a reason to love. He loves because He is love.

Moses said:

> The Lord did not set his affection on you and choose you because you were more numerous than other peoples, for you were the fewest of all peoples. But it was because the Lord loved you and kept the oath he swore to your forefathers that he brought you out with a mighty hand and redeemed you from the land of slavery, from the power of Pharaoh king of Egypt. (Deut. 7:7–8)

Men and women are relational beings, thinking beings, emotional beings and choosing beings. In possessing these four qualities, we are said to be in the image of God. God has these qualities and has communicated them to us. In all these things we are but a shadow; our capacity is limited, but God's capacity is unlimited. God relates perfectly, thinks correctly about everything, chooses appropriately and never experiences an emotional problem. Whatever He feels is motivated by love.

Created in the image of God, people were made to live in union with God, in dependence on Him, so that all our limitations might find their complement in the life of the Eternal. It is a great mistake to think of Adam and Eve, as we said earlier, as being created, then put in a position to rise or fall according to their own personality. It was more likely that it was a probationary period by which they could pass to a larger form of existence if they remained in union with God. If, however, they chose a separate existence, they would encompass their own ruin and would fall.

Thus in the garden of His activity, God marked the limits of His possibility by two sacramental symbols. Both were trees. One was the tree of life from which man could eat; the other, the tree of the knowledge of good and evil from which man was not to eat. The tree of life reminded Adam and Eve of their dependence on God for the sustenance of their life. Their wills were under test. They were sovereigns under Sovereignty. Independent yet dependent.

The will, in its attempt to secure mastership outside God, will never succeed. People ask, "Why is it that I don't have much will power?" Because of the Fall, human will will never function effectively unless it is brought back into correspondence with the divine will.

Tennyson put it like this:

> Our wills are ours, we know not how,
> Our wills are ours, to make them thine.

Each part has suffered in the effects of the Fall. When Adam and Eve introduced into human nature the principle of evil, it interrupted innocence and ruined it. Instead of the mind being clear and full of the knowledge of God, it became clouded. And instead of possessing that once-strong love for God, men became resentful of God and emotional wrecks, fragile and weak. And the once-obedient will became rebellious.

Adam and Eve's relationships were affected, their intelligence darkened, their emotions deadened, their will paralysed and their physical beings impaired. Darkened intelligence sees only the things that are near, looking at things as if semi-blind; deadened emotion will attempt to satisfy itself wholly within the realm of earth; and love set upon things that are material will be forever wounded.

A degraded will – ever attempting to be authoritative and masterful – will always be thwarted, always beaten, always overcome. Instead of clearly reflecting God, Adam and Eve were as broken lenses reflecting broken light. Fallen humanity, in this dire situation and desolate ruin, needs a Deliverer. Will one come?

Chapter 5

THE SPREAD OF
THE DISEASE

What God formed, sin deformed; that is the grim message of the two previous chapters. How consequential to the world was the damage that began with Adam and Eve's fall? That is the issue with which we come to grips in this chapter.

In an interesting article in *Things Which Become Sound Doctrine*, Dwight Pentecost discussed the question, How far did Adam fall? "Some," he says, believe Adam fell *upward* "so that Adam's lot was better after the Fall than before the Fall because something was added to the personality of Adam of which he had been deprived previously."

Others believe, he continued, that when Adam fell, he fell over the cliff; but when he was going over, he grabbed something and held on. "If he exerts enough will and enough strength, he can pull himself back up over the brink and stand on solid ground again." Those who have that concept, he pointed out, "are trying to lift themselves by their own bootstraps and work their way into heaven".

Scripture teaches that when Adam fell, he fell all the way. He became so depraved that he could do nothing to save himself or those who came after him. And those who came after him were as depraved as he. Here's how we can be sure of that fact.

DEPRAVITY PLAYED OUT IN HISTORY

No sooner do we leave the opening section of Genesis than we see the doubt, rebellion and suspicion of God's goodness, which arose in the hearts of Adam and Eve, playing itself out in history. The failure of the first human pair in the Garden of Eden plunged the world into a desperate situation. And the desperation has developed into a universal and cosmic catastrophe.

Let's look at the first of the tragic consequences that resulted from their primal sin. "There were many firsts in the opening chapter of Genesis," says Philip Yancey, in *Discovering God*, "the *first* man and woman, the *first* birth, the *first* division of labor, the *first* formal worship, the *first* extended family, the *first* city. But there is one *first* which overshadows all others – the *first* murder."

Here's how it happened. To Adam and Eve was born a son whose name was Cain. Later another son was born whom they named Abel. Cain kept to the fields and Abel kept to the sheep. There came a moment, however, when great conflict flared up between them because of a command God had given. The divine requirement was that they bring a blood offering to the Lord, which meant that they had to kill an animal. Cain decided not to do that.

This is how the biblical record puts it:

> *In the course of time Cain brought some of the fruits of the soil as an offering to the Lord. But Abel brought fat portions from some of the firstborn of his flock. The Lord looked with favour on Abel and his offering, but on Cain and his offering he did not look with favour. So Cain was very angry, and his face was downcast. Then the Lord said to Cain, "Why are you angry? Why is your face downcast? If you do what is right, will you not be accepted? But if you do not do what is right, sin is crouching at your door; it desires to have you, but you must master it."* (Gen. 4:3–7)

Cain took a knife and slit the throat of his brother as he had seen Abel kill the sheep. And apparently he wasn't even remorseful about it.

> *Now Cain said to his brother Abel, "Let's go out to the field." And while they were in the field, Cain attacked his brother Abel and killed him.* (Gen. 4:8)

Don't attempt to rationalise Cain's great sin by believing that he was merely a victim of the corruption that had entered his bloodstream by reason of his parents' transgressions. The anger that arose in his heart could have been brought under control *had he chosen to do so.*

Emotions may have a strong pull on us, but they cannot force us to commit a moral violation. Cain was certainly a victim of the corruption that was in his nature as a result of Adam and Eve's sin, but he became an agent, responsible for his actions, when he decided to undertake the murderous act. Make no mistake about it: Cain committed *premeditated* murder.

God, in fact, warned him about the murderous thought that was in his mind, when He said, "Sin is crouching at your door; it desires to have you, but you must master it" (4:7). Had he dealt with that thought while it was in his mind and expelled it, we would not be reading now the story of the world's first murder, probably the greatest relational sin that can ever be committed.

Inevitably and immediately divine judgment comes.

Then the Lord said to Cain, "Where is your brother Abel?" "I don't know," he replied. "Am I my brother's keeper?" The Lord said, "What have you done? Listen! Your brother's blood cries out to me from the ground. Now you are under a curse and driven from the ground, which opened its mouth to receive your brother's blood from your hand. When you work the ground, it will no longer yield its crops for you. You will be a restless wanderer on the earth." Cain said to the Lord, "My punishment is more than I can bear." (Gen. 4:9–13)

The sin of murder was not just limited to Cain. Later other murders and murderers followed. One was called Lamech. We read about it later on in Genesis 4:

Lamech said to his wives, "Adah and Zillah, listen to me; wives of Lamech, hear my words. I have killed a man for wounding me, a young man for injuring me. If Cain is avenged seven times, then Lamech seventy-seven times." (Gen. 4:23–24)

How could such evil things as murder and other sinful acts take place so early in the world's history? Because the same desires rose within people's hearts as in the hearts of Adam and Eve – the desire to take their own way, as opposed to the way of God.

And Genesis 5:1–3 gives us a special insight into this:

This is the written account of Adam's line. When God created man, he made him in the likeness of God. He created them male and female and blessed them. And when they were created, he called them "man". When Adam had lived 130 years, he had a son in his own likeness, in his own image; and he named him Seth.

Glance again at verse 1: "When God created man, he made him in the likeness of God." That's how God made Adam, in His own likeness. But then we read, "Adam ... had a son in his own image." God created Adam and Eve in *His* likeness. Adam and Eve created Cain in *their* likeness. The depravity that was inside them worked itself out in the next generation ... and the next ... and the next. The malignant results of the Fall spread throughout the whole human race.

Cain and Lamech acted in a murderous way because they allowed the evil thought that entered their minds to remain there unchallenged. Entertaining the thought led to a change in their feelings and ultimately in the decision of the will – a decision that tragically brought two human lives to an end.

The phrases "in the image" or "likeness of God" never occur in the Old Testament after the account of creation, save in the ninth chapter of the book of Genesis. Mankind is safeguarded from murder, the reason being that no one has a right to destroy something made in God's image (Gen. 9:6). By the act of sin, the image and likeness of God in humanity was not destroyed but defaced, and right through the history of the Old Testament it is seen as a degraded ideal.

Listen to how Dick Keyes put it in *Beyond Identity*:

A man is the image of God in his being however he may choose to use his abilities. A cruel and heartless man is as much the image of God in this sense as the man who is kind and loving, not because these qualities have nothing to do with the divine image but because he is ontologically (by his creation) the image of God irrespective of how he uses or misuses his gifts and abilities. Indeed the Bible shows that God puts great value on human beings even after they have rebelled against him. The value of any human being does not come from his goodness or creativity, his contribution to the state, the economy or the size of his bank account or even the number of his press clippings. His value is because he carries in his whole being the image of God.

The early chapters of Genesis tell of other changes that affected the world as a result of the first human beings choosing against their Creator. Suffering multiplied and a new word, *death*, entered the vocabulary. The word *death* (and associated words such as *die, dying, dead*) occur more than twenty times in the book of Genesis alone, and nearly a thousand times in the Bible as a whole. Perfection was permanently spoiled.

THE INEVITABLE SPIRAL

The downward cycle of rebellion continued until finally God reached a fateful decision. Genesis 6 records what must be one of the most poignant sentences of Scripture:

The Lord was grieved that he had made man on the earth, and his heart was filled with pain. (Gen. 6:6)

God, who had taken such pride in His creation, was now ready to destroy it. He would no longer tolerate the violence that had spread throughout the world. Then came the great Flood. You can read all about that in Genesis 7. These next verses set the scene for one of the greatest ecological disasters the world has ever known.

In the six hundredth year of Noah's life, on the seventeenth day of the second month – on that day all the springs of the great deep burst forth, and the floodgates of the heavens were opened. And rain fell on the earth for forty days and forty nights. (Gen. 7:11–12)

The first human beings made such a mess of things that God decided to start again. Only eight people survived the great Flood. Will a new start make a difference? Sadly, no. When we step out of Genesis 7 into the later chapters of this first book of the Bible, we find the same things occurring all over again – murder, lust, sin and rebellion.

In Genesis 19, we have the story of another environmental disaster, when once again God was so tired of rampant sin in the lives of those who lived in the twin cities of Sodom and Gomorrah that He decided to destroy all the inhabitants. Two messengers from God came and said:

> *"The outcry to the Lord against its people is so great that he has sent us to destroy it."* (Gen. 19:13)

Nothing could save Sodom and Gomorrah from God's indignation.

> *Then the Lord rained down burning sulphur on Sodom and Gomorrah – from the Lord out of the heavens. Thus he overthrew those cities and the entire plain, including all those living in the cities – and also the vegetation in the land.* (Gen. 19:24–25)

Clearly the human race was infected and affected with a disease far more dangerous than cancer or heart disease. Theologians call it "depravity". What exactly is depravity? The dictionary says that depravity is "the innate moral corruption of human nature".

A more theological definition of *depravity* is this: the desire to make our lives work independently of God. That definition takes us to the roots of the issue. Deeply embedded in human nature is a stubborn commitment to independence. One of the results of the Fall is that we don't like God telling us what to do. All of us carry this propensity within us.

One of the most powerful statements that shows us the extent of depravity can be seen by a glance at Genesis 6:5:

> *The Lord saw how great man's wickedness on the earth had become, and that every inclination of the thoughts of his heart was only evil all the time.*

Note the words "every inclination of the thoughts of his heart was only evil all the time". Not *occasionally* but *perpetually*. Every person on the face of planet Earth is a depraved human being. Line up some of the greatest personalities of the Old Testament, and they are all the same. All are flawed – Moses, Joshua, David. And the Bible doesn't airbrush these characters so that we see only their good side. The scars of sin are never hidden. Take King David for example.

KING DAVID'S SELF-DECEPTION

David was said to be a man after God's own heart, yet he is shown in the Bible to have committed two of the vilest sins in the book – adultery and murder. He coveted the wife of one of his captains. Then while the army was in the field fighting his battles, he seduced the woman and, then fearing exposure, plotted the death of her husband and added murder to treachery and lust.

We are a long way from Psalm 23 now. How could a man who was called the friend of God stoop so low? How indeed unless you accept the fact that depravity had invaded him.

When the tempter came, the man after God's own heart fell into sin. But that was not the worst. His sad reasoning led him to believe that he was innocent, and after he had married the woman, he thought that had rubbed out the sins of adultery and murder. He told himself that Uriah had died in the proper discharge of his duty, conveniently forgetting that he had given instructions to have him put in the hottest part of the battle. He was so self-deceived about his sin that he strutted about as if nothing had happened.

W.E. Sangster, the famous Methodist preacher in England throughout the first half of the twentieth century, had this to say about self-deception in *Why Jesus Never Wrote a Book:*

> Self deception, I suggest, is the worst state of mankind. Nothing exceeds its awfulness. It is a state of self deception that persuades us wrong is right. It is when men begin to call distinctions of right and wrong a matter of taste, when they call light darkness and darkness light and begin to believe it themselves. This induces a state of moral myopia so that they cannot see the issue clearly. They have so tampered with their conscience that it does not move with speed

and certainty and they resemble ships at sea with a faulty compass.

How did God bring home to David the reality of what he had done? He was saved by the prophet Nathan. The seer came to him and told him a simple story of a rich man with many flocks and herds who stole from a poor man his one little lamb and killed it. David was deeply moved by the story, but he was so self-deceived that he saw no application to himself. As soon as the story was finished, he rose in anger and said, "As surely as the Lord lives, the man who did this deserves to die!" (2 Sam. 12:5).

David had hardly got the words out of his mouth when the prophet's voice boomed out: "You are the man!" (v.7). The lie was exposed; the sophistry was at an end. We hear once more the David of the psalms as he cries:

Have mercy on me, O God, according to your unfailing love; according to your great compassion blot out my transgressions. Wash away all my iniquity and cleanse me from my sin. For I know my transgressions, and my sin is always before me. Against you, you only, have I sinned and done what is evil in your sight, so that you are proved right when you speak and justified when you judge ... Surely you desire truth in the inner parts; you teach me wisdom in the inmost place. Cleanse me with hyssop, and I shall be clean; wash me, and I shall be whiter than snow. (Psa. 51:1–4, 6–7)

Lest you live under the delusion that depravity was something only the Old Testament personalities struggled with, listen to what Jesus had to say to the scribes and Pharisees of His day:

"Woe to you, scribes and Pharisees, hypocrites! For you are like whitewashed tombs which indeed appear beautiful outwardly, but inside are full of dead men's bones and all uncleanness. Even so you also outwardly appear righteous to men, but inside you are full of hypocrisy and lawlessness." (Matt. 23:27–28, NKJV)

Repeatedly the Bible reminds us that we are morally depraved – all of us. Here are some pertinent texts:

For there is no-one who does not sin. (2 Chron. 6:36)

All have turned aside, they have together become corrupt; there is no-one who does good, not even one. (Psa. 14:3)

Even from birth the wicked go astray; from the womb they are wayward and speak lies. (Psa. 58:3)

Who can say, "I have kept my heart pure; I am clean and without sin"? (Prov. 20:9)

When the sentence for a crime is not quickly carried out, the hearts of the people are filled with schemes to do wrong. (Eccl. 8:11)

There is not a righteous man on earth who does what is right and never sins. (Eccl. 7:20)

For all have sinned and fall short of the glory of God. (Rom. 3:23)

Ian Macpherson, in his book *The Faith Once Delivered*, tells of an old Scottish preacher by the name of John Macrae who had a graphic word picture of mankind's moral predicament. "Compare," Macrae said, "the Christian in his perilous journey through this world to a man walking through a narrow passage between two rows of close fires with a sack of gun powder on his back. He must be careful at every step that he does not go nearer one side than the other lest the smallest spark of the fire should touch the powder and blow him to pieces."

NO ONE IS EXEMPT

The Bible goes to great lengths to show us that we have inherited from Adam and Eve a nature which has a bias towards evil. As Thomas Adams put it in his neat aphorism, "Iniquity can plead antiquity". Take these texts for example:

Your first father sinned; your spokesmen rebelled against me. (Isa. 43:27)

Sin entered the world through one man. (Rom. 5:12)

Sin that dwells in me (Rom. 7:17, NKJV).

"It's all this stuff about original sin that I can't swallow," said a sceptic to Seth Joshua, a famous Welsh preacher. "You don't have to swallow it," he answered. "It's already inside you."

Depravity, this hidden source of pollution that is in us, is passed on from one generation to another. Dwight Pentecost cites the report of a crime commission in America a number of years ago:

> Every baby starts life as a little savage. He is completely selfish and self centered. He wants what he wants when he wants it – his bottle, his mother's attention, his playmate's toy, his uncle's watch. Deny him these once, and he seethes with rage and aggressiveness, which would be murderous were he not so helpless. He is in fact, dirty. He has no morals, no knowledge, no skills. This means that all children – not just certain children – are born delinquent. If permitted to continue in the self centered world of his infancy, given free reign to his impulsive actions to satisfy his wants, every child would grow up a criminal, a thief, a killer or a rapist.

The fact that we have a sinful nature is surely self-evident. Always and everywhere it is easier to do wrong than right just as it is easier to walk downhill than uphill. If there were no record of the Fall, it would be necessary to invent one to account for mankind's moral condition.

In this connection Margaret Wilkinson wrote:

I never cut my neighbour's throat
    My neighbour's purse I never stole;
I never spoiled his house and lands,
    But God have mercy on my soul!
For I am haunted night and day
    By all the deeds I have not done
That unattempted loveliness
    O, costly valour never won!

As we watch the manner in which the tempter came to Eve in Genesis 3, surely we must recognise that this is not just a story that comes to us out of the ancient past; it's as up-to-date as the temptation you faced last night, the temptation you may be feeling this morning, the temptation you face in your study, in your home, in your ministry, in your life. The scene has changed, but the methodology has not.

Cast your mind back once more to how the primal sin took place. Adam and Eve had everything they needed back there in the garden, but there came a moment of temptation when one thought dominated their minds: Are we missing out on something? Is God keeping something from us? They failed to resist that temptation – the temptation to reach out and take something that was forbidden to them – and began a slide that affects every one of us to this very day.

Some theologians have likened depravity to a congenital disease. The predisposition is there from earliest infancy. It is infectious; no quarantine can effectively prescribe or limit its incidence. It is disfiguring; it destroys the image so that God cannot see His reflection in us. And it is fatal in its consequences. "Sin, when it is full-grown, brings forth death" (James 1:15, NKJV).

John Newton offers a lyrical compendium of the range of resemblances between depravity and disease:

> The worst of all diseases
>   Is light compared with sin
> On every part it seizes
>   But rages most within.
> 'Tis leprosy and fever
>   And palsy all combined
> And none but the believer
>   The least relief can find.

OUR GREATEST ALLY
IN THE FIGHT AGAINST DEPRAVITY

We ought never to run away with the idea that we are just helpless victims of depravity and are powerless to do anything about it. God has built within us a conscience, which is one of our greatest allies when we wish to fight against our innate depravity.

Conscience never takes time off. It can, however, be easily stifled or smothered. It tells us we should do right, but it cannot always tell us what is right to do. Etymologically the word *conscience* means "knowledge with oneself" or "complete knowledge." Theologically it means more. Archbishop Trench, one of Britain's great arch-bishops, defined *conscience* in this way: "I know that God knows that I know." Alexander MacDol, a Scottish preacher, said: "Conscience is the supreme court of the universe set up in the human spirit."

Conscience is not an infallible guide. It needs sensitising, enlightening, reinforcing. Hugh Redwood, a journalist, said, "Your conscience is a watchdog, but make sure you don't feed it sleeping tablets." Conscience, guided by the truths of Scripture and energised by the grace of God, becomes a powerful spiritual force in the battle against inner corruption.

All this contradicts some common assumptions about human history. There are those who say that over the millennia we have been evolving to a better state. But look around and what do you see? People murder, lust, and a whole host of things. What happened in Eden is with us today.

The world has never been the same. The disease has spread over all the world and has infected every one of earth's inhabitants. Every generation needs regeneration. Sin has touched everyone and no one is exempt. Every part of us has been infected – physically, emotionally, mentally, volitionally and relationally.

The emphasis I am making on the subject of human depravity must not cause us to overlook the fact that though we are victims of depravity, we still carry within us a likeness to God. That gives us dignity.

In *Being a Responsible Christian in a Non-Christian Society*, John Stott writes:

We human beings have both a unique dignity as creatures made in God's image and a unique depravity as sinners under his judgment. The former gives us hope, the latter places a limit on our expectations. Our Christian critique of the secular mind is that it tends to be either too naively optimistic or too negatively pessimistic in its estimates of the human condition, whereas the Christian mind firmly rooted in biblical realism, both celebrates the glory and deplores the shame of our human being. We can behave like God in whose image we are made only to descend to the level of the beasts. We are able to think choose, create, love and worship, but also refuse to think, to choose evil, to destroy, to hate and to worship ourselves. We build churches and drop bombs. We develop intensive care units for the critically ill and use the same technology to torture political enemies who presume to disagree with us. This is "man" – a strange bewildering paradox, dust of earth and breath of God, shame and glory.

THE THEATRES OF WAR

The problem of depravity deepens when we consider that not only have we inherited a fallen nature but we also live in a fallen world. The world around us – our physical universe – has been adversely affected by Adam and Eve's sin. A curse fell upon the whole of creation and now is here with us. Ours is a beautiful world, but it has been spoiled. Everything that lives is subject to disease –

animals, birds, fish, flowers. Life seems strangely poisoned. The woman who wrote the beautiful hymn *All Things Bright and Beautiful* was being selective. She didn't write of the horrible things in nature. She wasn't seeing the whole of it. But Paul did! When he looked at creation, he looked at all of it and held his faith in the face of awful problems. A close observer and an honest man, he said:

The whole creation groans. (Rom. 8:22, NKJV)

In the middle years of the nineteenth century, there was a sharp controversy between philosophers and theologians over man's perfectability. The philosophers were saying that man is on the way to becoming perfect on his own. They thought there was some ethical evolution at work in our race, unrelated to any particular religion. Herbert Spencer said, "Man *must* become perfect."

The theologians, who at that time seemed to be having the worst of the argument, claimed, as did the apostle Paul, that man is carnal, "sold under sin" (Rom. 7:14, AV). That was 150 years ago. Now that argument is heard no more. There is no escalator to perfection. There is no mechanical progress. We look back and see that almost every discovery of science has been twisted to devilish use. We are muddied creatures.

Then there is the devil. One of the characters in Dylan Thomas's *Under Milk Wood* says, "I want to be good but nobody will let me." One of those who would not let him was of course the devil. Scripture says:

Your enemy the devil prowls around like a roaring lion looking for someone to devour. (1 Pet. 5:8)

Of course, many do not believe in a personal devil. I have met some Christians who hold this view. They say that references to the devil in Scripture are about an evil influence rather than an evil intelligence. But the names given to him in Scripture predicate personality: Satan, deceiver, liar, murderer, tempter, the evil one, and so on. The devil is a personal, aggressive, evil, intelligent being who has to be reckoned with seriously and vigilantly. These words summarise perfectly the thoughts I am trying to convey:

> Men don't believe in the devil now,
>   As their fathers used to do.
> They reject one creed because it's old,
>   for another because it's new.
> But who dogs the steps of the toiling saint,
>   who spreads the net for his feet?
> Who sows the tares in the world's broad fields,
>   where the Saviour sows His wheat?
> People may say the devil never lived,
>   they may say the devil has gone,
> But simple people would like to know –
>   who carries his business on?

Inevitably, this combination of factors – a fallen nature, an environment affected by sin and a malevolent devil – mean that we are surrounded on all sides by temptation.

Before we leave this issue of how the disease of depravity has spread throughout the universe, it is important to understand that the Bible, when affirming the fact of human corruption, is not saying that man is totally bad in the sense he can do no good or perform a good act. To suggest that would be to fly in the face of reality. Nor does the Bible want to suggest that God is indifferent to the good that is done to help people who are suffering. What it says is this: that goodness cannot save us. It gets in the way of God's grace and so prevents us from accepting Christ as Saviour.

To quote John Stott again:

> This doctrine has suffered from many mis-conceptions, for the average person would define total depravity by saying that man is as bad as he can be. However, if we adopt that as an acceptable definition immediately our theology is brought into question because we know men who are not as bad as they can be. We know many men who are good men, kind men, generous men, moral men, men who contribute much in the home and in the community. Rather the doctrine of depravity says that man is as bad off as he can be. There is a vast difference between being as bad as he can be and being as bad off as he can be.

So the disease continues. Instead of adoring God, we fight with Him. Instead of believing what He said, we reject His truth. Instead of doing what He wants us to do, we delight in doing what He doesn't want us to do. We cover it up and we repeat the mistake of Adam and Eve all over again.

Lest you live under the delusion that sin affected only Adam and Eve, then consider your own life. Why do you do the things you do? Call to mind your impulses, your problems, the secret motives that you alone know.

Mark Twain said, "Everybody is a moon and has a dark side which he never shows to anybody." The slide into depravity – the desire to run our lives on our own terms without recourse to God – has affected every individual who has ever been born, with the single exception of Jesus Christ. We all have within us the propensity to do evil and to disobey the Word of God because we doubt His goodness and rebel against His love.

We can't help having caught the disease, but we can combat it by drawing upon the grace of God that enables us to rise above the influences that depravity has brought into our lives.

To minimise the malady is to detract from the marvel of the remedy. This is why Scripture so surgically probes the nature of sin. The more serious its diagnosis of the character of evil, the more marvellous the salvation it offers as a sole cure. Before we consider the wonder of that salvation, however, we must focus on the dynamics of problem development – how problems arise in our personality and how they are maintained. To that subject we turn next.

Chapter 6

HOW PROBLEMS DEVELOP

Having seen something of the design of God for our personalities – to be bearers of the divine image – and how that image has been defaced and deformed, we now have a theological framework for understanding how problems arise in the personality.

Had we tried to address the process of problem development without comprehending how things went so badly wrong (from a biblical perspective) it might have exposed us to what has been described as "the evangelical disease" – giving answers before we fully understand the problem.

Humanistic psychology provides us with many different explanations for the process of problem development, but no secular textbook on psychology can compete with the fuller and more rounded clarification of Scripture. Our personal problems have long roots that go back to the depravity we inherited from the first human pair.

To begin understanding how problems develop, let's take a problem that most of us have struggled with at one time or another – *extreme anxiety*. You may be struggling with this right now. Something has happened that fills your mind with such concern that you are unable to concentrate on your daily tasks or routine responsibilities. Your mind turns things over and over, and soon your imagination gets to work magnifying the problem and increasing your anxiety.

As a pastor and counsellor, I have a healthy respect for the imagination. Some psychologists regard the imagination as ten times more powerful than the will. They believe that if the will is set in one direction but the imagination is set in another, the imagination will ultimately win. I am talking here, of course, about the negative power of imagination; it has a positive place in the personality as well.

Negative imagination boosts anxiety; it says, "This situation is likely to go from bad to worse." Soon your anxiety grows into a spectre that haunts your mind and enslaves your whole personality.

As a Christian, you know that God is in control of all things, that Christ lives in you and that all things work together for good to them that love God. You know all that in your head, but most of us live not from the head but from the heart. When negative imagination takes control, you live as if God is no longer in control of the situation and that all His promises about being a Rock and Refuge in time of trouble have little relationship to your problem.

Some Christians attempt to anaesthetise the pain of increasing anxiety by a quick fix, like raiding the refrigerator, watching a movie, masturbating, drinking alcohol to excess, going on a shopping spree, jogging, making endless phone calls or cleaning the house from top to bottom. Some of these are legitimate means of escape from internal pressures, providing they do not violate the trust and confidence in God.

David Powlinson, in the *Journal of Biblical Counseling*, described the state of believers who hold on to one thing in their heads but another in their hearts:

> You live as if some temporary good feeling could provide you refuge, as if your actions could make the world right. Your functional god competes with your professed God ... faith professes, sings and prays one way, but when push comes to shove, trusts something else.

If we are to live a life that is continually empowered by Christ and not by our own "functional gods", we must have a clear grasp of how problems arise in the first place. And we must understand them from a *biblical* point of view.

In stressing the world *biblical* I am not anti-psychology. I simply believe that Scripture can give us more complete and reliable answers to human problems than the best secular textbooks on the subject of the human psyche. If there were no psychology, we would not be at a loss to understand the rise and development of human problems, providing we open the Scriptures.

Here's a text I always refer my students to in my opening lectures on counselling:

> *"The heart is deceitful above all things and beyond cure. Who can understand it? I the Lord search the heart and examine the mind, to reward a man according to his conduct, according to what his deeds deserve."* (Jer. 17:9–10)

If, as Scripture says, God alone knows the heart, then it follows that if we are to understand what has gone wrong, we must first and foremost pay attention to God's revelation of the human condition. So with God's Word as our guide, let's build a biblical framework for understanding problem development. At the risk of oversimplification, I want to suggest just five basic causes of behaviour.

HOW THE PHYSICAL AFFECTS THE PSYCHOLOGICAL

"We are having a prayer meeting in our church for my son one night next week," the caller said. "He is demon-possessed, and I would greatly value your prayers that God will deliver him."

I said I was reluctant to pray over such a matter when I had not been involved in the diagnosis, so invited her to bring the child to see me. When we met, I asked who made the diagnosis and the circumstances behind it. She had attended a series of evangelistic services in her church, and because she had no one to look after her little boy, age four, she took him with her to the services.

The child apparently found it difficult to sit still anywhere and at times would break away from his mother and run out into the aisle of the church. On the last night of the evangelistic series, the young child broke away from his mother and ran down the aisle towards the pulpit when the evangelist was preaching. The mother immediately left her seat to collect the child, and as she did so, the evangelist stopped preaching and said, "That child is demon-possessed."

At the close of the meeting, the church elders met with the evangelist and asked for his advice in dealing with the situation. "Have the most spiritual Christians meet together one night," he said. "Put the child in the midst and proceed to cast out the evil spirit in the Name of Jesus."

After I had talked to the child for half an hour, it was clear that he was not demon-possessed. I took a history of the child's birth and development and soon realised that the child was hyperactive. I became suspicious that he might be suffering from a physical problem and arranged immediately for him to see a doctor friend of mine who within a few days had diagnosed a small degree of brain damage.

The doctor telephoned me a few days later and said, "I have put the child on appropriate medication, and there is a definite improvement. I agree with you; there is no evidence of demonic possession, but there is evidence of physiological malfunction."

When the church leaders heard this, they immediately cancelled the proposed exorcism and came to see me to discuss the matter further. They expressed appreciation for my intervention. One said, "I dread to think what damage we might have done to that little child by suggesting to him that his body might be the host to an evil spirit."

Physical causes may underlie behaviour problems. Physically we have all been affected by the Fall. Because of the curse that fell on Adam and Eve, no human body functions perfectly. A doctor friend of mine told me there are 120 things that can go wrong with the thumb! And a malfunctioning physiology can quickly affect the way we think and feel, adding to the difficulties with the pain of upset emotions.

I learned early in my counselling ministry to have respect for the physical causes that might lie behind behaviour. A virus, for example, can produce depression. Allergies can affect and influence a person's behaviour. Significant sleep loss can produce hallucinations. Depression can be caused by chemical factors in the body as well as by outside factors such as loss, absence of meaning in one's life or family difficulties.

Here's another example that illustrates the need to ensure that emotional or seemingly spiritual problems are not the result of some physiological malfunction. A deacon asked my help "to explore why I feel so thoroughly backslidden and indolent in my soul". He added: "I don't want to pray or read the Bible, and I've lost all desire for my daily quiet time with the Lord." I said I was willing to explore the possibilities of what might be happening in his life but first asked him to have a medical checkup.

His doctor discovered he was suffering from hypoglycaemia, or low blood sugar. Appropriate medication had him looking like a new man within days. His problem was rooted not in a lack of spirituality but in his physiology.

One of the principles by which I have operated in the fifty years I have been involved in Christian counselling is this: when people have come to me with serious emotional problems, I have insisted that they first have a medical checkup.

A principle I have learned in the field of counselling is this: when trying to help people with their problems, it is sometimes necessary to eliminate the physical as a cause. Counsellors who ignore the fact that there can be physical causes for behaviour can do more harm than good.

It is equally true, of course, that emotional or spiritual problems can affect us physically. Problems in the soul can off-load themselves onto the body. The medical fraternity has come up with a beautiful word to describe this phenomenon – *psychosomatic*. It is made up of two Greek words, *psyche* meaning "soul" and *soma* meaning "body."

Some time ago I listened to John Sarno on *Larry King Live*. Dr Sarno, widely respected in the medical field, treats people with back trouble. I bought his book in which he makes the astonishing claim that the usual kind of back pain can be stopped forever without drugs, exercise or surgery. Most back problems, he claims, are the result of emotions off-loading themselves onto the body. Although some people may have structural faults, the major cause of back pain is due to emotional factors – particularly repressed anger.

In his book *Healing Back Pain*, Sarno explained:

> Pain syndromes look so "physical" it is particularly difficult for doctors to consider the possibility that they might be caused by psychological factors, and so they cling to the structural explanation. In doing so, however, they are chiefly responsible for the pain epidemic that now exists in the country. ... There are those in medicine who believe that emotions play a role in all aspects of health and illness. I am one of them. I believe that all medical studies are flawed if they do not consider the emotional factor. For example, a research project dealing with the hardening of the arteries usually included consideration of diet (cholesterol) weight, exercise, genetic factors – but if it does not include emotional factors, the results in my view are not valid.

No sharp distinction can be drawn between the soul and the body. The soul doesn't live within the body as a kernel exists within a shell of a nut. Soul and body are intertwined in a way not yet fully understood, but each acts and reacts upon the other. Certain desires can be said to belong to the body – sexual desires, for example. They are divine in origin and come to us as powerful instincts. If they were to cease to function, it would mean that our race would vanish from the earth.

Sadly, in both counselling and medicine, diagnoses are made every day that do not take into account the whole of human functioning.

The first key then for understanding how problems may arise in the personality is uncorrected physical disorders.

RELATIONAL ISSUES
AFFECTING BEHAVIOUR

A young woman once came to me to ask for my help. She was struggling with a perceived lack of femininity. I noticed that her hair was cut short and she was wearing a man's shirt. It was obvious before she spoke that she was doing a really good job concealing the fact she was a woman.

After I asked how I could help, her opening words were these: "For some reason I have lost touch with my femininity. I hate being a woman, and yet I know this is how God has designed me. I need help in getting in touch with the feminine side of my nature."

She then told me about the sexual abuse she had received at the hands of her father. For several years she wondered if this kind of thing happened to every young girl in a family, but when one day she confided in a friend what was happening, she was horrified to discover that what she was experiencing was not just unusual but depraved.

She left home, broke with her family, and eventually won for herself a place in one of Britain's universities. While there she became a Christian, and the more she began to understand about the Christian faith, the more she realised that she needed to talk to someone about her difficulties. She offered these reflections: "I think I might be saying deep down inside me things like this: When all I had to offer was my femininity, my own father took advantage of me. So I began to conceal it so that I would never again be abused."

Several sessions later, and feeling concerned that we didn't appear to be making much progress, I remarked that whenever she talked about her abusive father she clenched her fists. My exact words were these: "I notice that your fists are clenched as you talk to me about your abuse. Am I right in assuming that if Jesus Christ walked into this room at this moment you would punch Him in the face?" I knew this was a risky statement to make, but I felt strangely impressed to make it.

A look of horror came over her. "How can you say such a thing?" she protested. "I would never do anything like that to Jesus Christ! I'm astonished that you would even suggest it." Then after a few minutes of silence, she said: "Now if my father walked into this room at this moment, I might well do that to him. But to Jesus? Never."

I paused for a few moments and then said quietly: "But Jesus let it happen." It took several minutes for the meaning to dawn on her. Then sitting back, with her fists still clenched, she said, "Yes, you are right. He did let it happen, and deep down I suppose my anger is against Him more than against my father."

She dropped to her knees and with copious tears poured out her heart to God in prayer, telling Him how much she hated Him for letting her father abuse her. Then, without any prompting from me, she asked God to forgive the hatred she had towards Him, a hatred buried deep inside her but never admitted. It was a dramatic moment, one of the most memorable in the whole of my counselling experience.

Our sessions took a different turn after that as she came to see that her problem was deeper than her relationship with her father. Her real difficulty was reconciling what had happened with the goodness of God. A lot of work was needed and a lot of hours spent in bringing her to the place where she could confess that God was good, even though she could not understand why He did not intervene to stop her father abusing her. Once the conviction took root in her heart that God was good, the new relationship she had with God transformed her relationship with her family and also with herself.

Underlying that woman's problem was a much deeper problem than the problem of sexual abuse. I do not wish in any way to minimise the father's responsibility. His actions were vile, irresponsible, depraved and deserved condemnation. But while she entertained in her heart a concept of God as being disinterested in her welfare, she would never be able to trust Him and receive from Him the grace she needed to overcome her problem. How can you trust a God of whom you are unsure?

The longings for relationship that God had built into her – for an intimate relationship with Him, with others and also with herself – had never been fully satisfied. Until the problem of lack of confidence in God was resolved, the relationship with others and with herself would never be fully satisfactory. Shut off from a close relationship with God, she was shut off from others and shut off from herself.

Behaviour can have relational causes. Assuming a problem does not have a physical basis, the next area to consider is relational. In fact, based on my own experience, almost every problem we face in life, if it is not physiologically based, will have within it a relational component. It will have something to do with our inability to relate well to God, to others or to ourselves.

Relationships do not so much cause problems as reveal problems. If we try to solve a non-organic problem without looking at the issue of relationships, then we will never fully resolve the difficulty.

It is worth considering again the statement of D. Broughton Knox to which I referred in Chapter 1:

> We learn from the Trinity that relationship is the essence of reality and therefore the essence of our existence.

If that statement is true, and I believe it is, then something more than such things as managing anger, acquiring better self-esteem, reinforcing will power, and examining self-talk needs to be considered when we seek to understand why we do what we do. Not that some of these issues do not have a place (examining self-talk for example), but something deeper is going on that needs our primary consideration.

Many Christian counsellors do not consider the relational aspect of our beings and, though they may help people function, they miss the opportunity to bring healing to the deepest part of the personality. "Nothing will touch our hearts to thrill it or break it like relationships," say John Eldridge and Brent Curtis in *The Sacred Romance*.

WHY AM I SO THIRSTY?

God has built into us a desire for relationship with Him, which if not satisfied leaves us open and vulnerable to other sources of satisfaction. If God is not satisfying our souls, we will seek something else to satisfy us. It is here that our personal problems begin.

This desire for relationship with God is described in the Bible by many words – *desire, hunger, longings,* but perhaps the most descriptive of these words is *thirst*. The Bible often uses this word to describe the desire God has given us for Himself.

In his book *The Pleasures of God*, John Piper tells of reading this statement in Henry Scougal's *The Life of God in the Soul of Man*:

> The soul of man ... hath in it a raging and inextinguishable thirst. Never does a soul know what solid joy and substantial pleasure is, till, once being weary of itself, it renounces all property [and] gives itself up to the Author of its being.

John Piper comments that as he read those words,

> There was in me an immense longing to give myself up to God, for the quenching of this "raging thirst".

Our hearts thirst for something that earth cannot satisfy. God created mankind with a desire to relate to Him and others. Men and women fundamentally are relational beings. We desire to reach out for the kind of relationship that enables us to feel good. Nothing satisfies so much as relationship. We yearn for someone to care for us, to satisfy the deep longings of our soul.

W.E. Sangster told this story in *Can I Know God?*

> There is an old legend of the Western Isles [of Scotland] concerning a sea king who desired the company of a human being. One day he heard in his cavern under the sea, a little human cry, and rose to the surface of the water to discover a child in a derelict boat. Just as he was about to make for the little vessel and take the child, a rescue party intervened, and he missed his prize. But, so the legend says, as they drew away with the one so nearly lost, the sea king cupped his hand and threw into the heart of the child a little sea-salt wave and said, as he submerged, "The child is mine. When it grows, the salt sea will call him and he will come home to me at the last." It is only a Gaelic legend, but it enshrines the timeless truth, God has put in the heart of everyone of us a longing for himself.

Solomon, in the book of Ecclesiastes, says something similar when he reinforces that important truth in these words:

He has also set eternity in the hearts of men. (Eccl. 3:11)

Most people do not understand this. They thirst for something, but they know not what. There is a longing in the soul, a thirst for relationships that is powerful, that though hidden, ignored, overlaid and even denied, has a powerful pull in our personalities. These longings are there because we were built to relate first to God and then to others. When we don't function in this way, then deep down we sense a high degree of spiritual discomfort because we are not relating to God and others in the way we were designed.

It is impossible for people to have a clear sense of their identity – who they really are – outside of a relationship with God. To paraphrase the famous words of the fourth-century preacher, Augustine: "We were made by God, and made for God, and our identity will never be fully complete until we relate to God."

Identity depends on three things – a sense that one is unconditionally loved, a sense of one's value, and a sense of meaning and purpose. Those three elements can well be described by these alliterative words – *security, self-worth* and *significance*. As these three words can mean different things to different people, let me define exactly how I am using them.

SECURITY

By *security* I mean the positive feelings that flood the soul when we know that we are loved and loved unconditionally. Everyone longs to be loved – with a love that will never be taken away. The more conscious we are that we are the objects of that kind of love, the easier it is to face up to life and rise above all its problems.

Years ago Frank Sinatra sang a song with these words: "You are nobody until somebody loves you." How true. The more aware I am that God loves me – and loves me unconditionally – the easier it is for me to do my daily tasks and relate well to others. People have often come into my counselling room and said, "My problem is that I don't love the Lord enough." My usual response to that statement is: "No, that is not your problem. Your problem is you don't know how much the Lord loves you." Then I tell this story:

Early in my Christian life I felt that because God was allowing all sorts of problems to crowd into my life, He couldn't really love me. One day I knelt before Him in prayer and said, rather petulantly I am afraid, "God, you don't love me." I stayed on my knees for some time, and there came into my mind a picture I had seen of Christ upon the cross with His arms outstretched and over the cross the caption "I love you this much". Instantly the scales seemed to fall from my eyes; and realising how much I was loved, my love for Him flamed in response. For the first time in my life, I understood the meaning of the apostle John's words, "We love because he first loved us" (1 John 4:19).

Our love for Christ is not something we manufacture in our hearts; it is the consequence of His love for us. His unconditional love touches the capacity to love in our hearts, and we find ourselves giving love for love. The kind of love for which our souls crave is divine love – love that goes on loving us no matter what. And that kind of love must flood our souls if we are to function the way we were designed and experience deep inner security.

SELF-WORTH

Another thing the soul needs in order to feel "at home" is a sense of self-worth. By *self-worth* I mean a sense of being valued. At first it may appear that the distinction between being loved and being valued is nonexistent. Think of it like this: When we are loved by someone, we feel cherished; when we are valued by someone, we feel worthwhile. Seeing how worthwhile we are in someone else's eyes contributes greatly to our own sense of worth.

One of the statements I learned when I was studying adolescent psychology was this: I am not what I think I am; I am not what you think I am; I am what I think you think I am. A child comes to sense how much he or she is valued not by what the parents (or those responsible for nurture) think, but by what *the child thinks* the parents think of the child. Often I have talked to young people whose parents loved them, but sadly somehow the message that they valued them did not get through. Hence they valued themselves not as their parents saw them but as they perceived their parents saw them. The self is a series of reflected appraisals. We value ourselves as we believe we are valued.

SIGNIFICANCE

Another thing the soul needs to feel at home is *significance*. By this I mean a sense of meaning and purpose. Every single person on the face of this earth has a purpose in being here. We are not just meteorites on our way across the universe to burn out on the edge of some gravitational field. We are men and women made in the image of God with the signature of God in our souls. No one has a purposeless existence on this earth, let alone a child of God. But we can only realise that purpose as we relate to God and hear Him say:

> *"For I know the plans I have for you," declares the Lord, "plans to prosper you and not to harm you, plans to give you hope and a future."* (Jer. 29:11)

"The search for meaning," said Victor Frankl, the Viennese psychiatrist who survived the horrors of a World War II concentration camp, "is one of the greatest pursuits of the human heart." Frankl built a whole system of psychotherapy on the concept that once we begin to see even a glimmer of meaning in our life, then something powerful happens to us.

He tells, in one of his books, how he helped a young unmarried mother who had been abandoned by her lover and who wanted to give up her child for adoption. Frankl counselled her: Think of the input you can make into this child's life, how you can prepare him for the destiny that has been built into him. Consider how you and you alone are the only one who can steer him to his fullest potential. When the young mother saw what Victor Frankl was saying and grasped the idea, she found meaning in life and became a new woman.

Come back with me once more to the story of Adam and Eve in their sinless state in the Garden of Eden. Picture them if you will standing on a firm and sturdy three-legged stool. Now give names to each one of those legs: security, self-worth and significance. Adam and Eve, because of their close and intimate relationship with God, knew what it meant to be unconditionally loved, highly valued, and for their lives to have total meaning. They would have felt secure, worthwhile and significant. (See illustration 1.)

Illustration 1

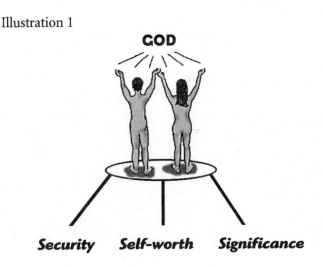

Security   Self-worth   Significance

When they sinned and their relationship with God was severed, however, it was as if they stepped off the firm stool on which they were standing and instead found themselves on shifting sand where security became insecurity, self-worth became inferiority, and significance became insignificance. Thus took place the world's first identity crisis. (See illustration 2.)

Illustration 2

Insecurity, Inferiority, Insignificance

Since the Fall, everyone born into this world arrives with a deep sense of insecurity, inferiority and insignificance. No human love can give us what our souls long for; and bereft of a relationship with God, the best that earthly relationships (such as parents, friends and peers) can do is to make us feel only moderately secure, worthwhile and significant. We will never resolve the identity crisis in our souls until we know how to relate to the true God who alone can give us what our souls require – unconditional love and eternal meaning.

We all long to get back to what was lost in the Garden of Eden. And our longings are the most powerful part of our personalities. Our longing fuels our search for meaning, for wholeness, for a sense of being truly alive. It is the most important thing about us, our heart of hearts, the passion of our life. And the voice that calls to us from this place is the voice of God. (See illustration 3.)

Illustration 3

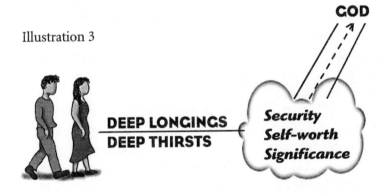

DEEP LONGINGS
DEEP THIRSTS

{ *Security*
Self-worth
Significance

GOD

This thirst in our souls, if not satisfied in God, lies behind most of the problems of the personality. Take almost any psychological problem and, when you cut your way through all the labels psychologists give to the various conditions, you come to a person who does not feel deeply loved, or who has little or no sense of worth, or feels there is no meaning or purpose to his or her life. Problems arise when we try to meet the deep needs of our souls outside of God.

If we do not drink deeply of the water that comes from Christ, then we will turn easily to other sources of satisfaction. This is how obsessions and compulsions occur. Things like habitual masturbation, pornography and overeating have a tremendous appeal for us, when our spirits lack the joy and pleasure that comes from Jesus Christ.

The Trinity designed our inner beings for the most incredible joy and satisfaction; but when we do not experience a close and intimate relationship with the Father, Son and Holy Spirit, then we become extremely vulnerable to those things that excite our senses and we find ourselves living for them or depending on them to satisfy our soul.

The second key to understanding how problems arise, then, is unsatisfied deep longings. No theory of how problems arise in the personality is complete until it takes into consideration all aspects of human functioning. More needs to be understood than that we are physical and relational beings. We are also beings who can think, feel and choose. We must now consider those parts of our personality.

Chapter 7

THERE'S MORE

Whatever is meant by that elusive term *person*, we mean someone who is a physical being, who can relate, think, feel and choose. We have been saying problems can arise because of physical malfunction and unsatisfied deep longings. If God is not meeting the deep ache in our hearts for a relationship with Him in which we feel secure, significant and worthwhile, then we will seek to have that ache satisfied in some other direction.

Consider now with me the third area of human functioning, our ability to think. How and what we think determines the direction we will go to have our thirst quenched. (See illustration 4.) There can be rational causes behind behaviour.

Illustration 4

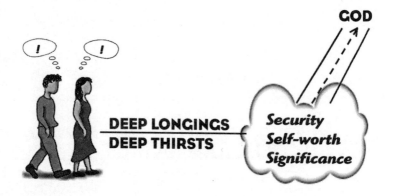

This ache we all feel in our hearts for a vertical relationship is not something God condemns. He designed us that way in the first place. What God condemns is the foolish and pointless ways we go about trying to satisfy that ache. And these foolish and pointless ways have their origins in the mind.

Our minds have been enemy territory since we arrived in this world. Satan, through the Fall, has established a bridgehead in our minds and continuously sends his envoys across it to militate against the influences of the Trinity.

This is how the apostle Paul put it in 2 Corinthians 4:4:

The god of this age has blinded the minds of unbelievers, so that they cannot see the light of the gospel of the glory of Christ, who is the image of God.

Later in the same epistle, the great apostle said:

But I am afraid that just as Eve was deceived by the serpent's cunning, your minds may somehow be led astray from your sincere and pure devotion to Christ. (2 Cor. 11:3)

When writing to the Ephesians, Paul put it like this:

So I tell you this, and insist on it in the Lord, that you must no longer live as the Gentiles do, in the futility of their thinking. They are darkened in their understanding and separated from the life of God because of the ignorance that is in them due to the hardening of their hearts. (Eph. 4:17–18)

Not everyone is willing to admit that their mind is one of Satan's strongholds. "What is wrong with my mind?" they say. "I am a perfectly normal and rational person." But there is a world of difference between what the world accepts as normal and what the Scriptures teach is normal.

In the world it is accepted as normal for a person to harbour resentment, to have periods of ill temper, to live together outside marriage, or look after number one. None of these things belong to the Christian life. The New Testament claims that by the power of the indwelling Christ, life can be lived above all these wrong humours – and lived without strain.

When Adam and Eve rebelled against God, the result of believing the lie that they could be more fulfilled by acting independently of God, they plunged every one of their descendants into moral darkness. There is now a blindness in our minds. Though it does not prevent us from understanding scientific laws, mathematics or any of the other things our educational establishments teach us, when we try to comprehend the moral and spiritual world, we reveal our mental failure.

EVERYONE IS A FOOL

The Bible uses an interesting word to describe our mental failure to figure out the moral world. It is called folly or foolishness. The book of Proverbs has a lot to say about fools and foolishness.

> *The way of a fool seems right to him, but a wise man listens to advice.* (Prov. 12:15)

> *A fool finds no pleasure in understanding but delights in airing his own opinions.* (Prov. 18:2)

> *Folly is bound up in the heart of a child, but the rod of discipline will drive it far from him.* (Prov. 22:15)

A fool in Proverbs is not someone who is intellectually challenged. A fool is someone who *thinks* he knows where life is to be found but doesn't. And a child in whose heart folly resides (as our last text put it) may well be able to relate to other areas of life with a degree of wisdom, but when it comes to moral issues and behaving as God requires us to behave, mental bankruptcy will be revealed.

King David, in one of his psalms, wrote this:

The fool says in his heart, "There is no God." They are corrupt, their deeds are vile; there is no-one who does good. The Lord looks down from heaven on the sons of men to see if there are any who understand, any who seek God. All have turned aside, they have together become corrupt; there is no-one who does good, not even one. (Psa. 14:1–3)

Here's the issue in a nutshell: Every one of us comes into the world with the foolish idea that life can be found through our own resources and our own efforts. God says it can't. We think we know better.

WHERE OUR FOOLISH STRATEGIES TAKE US

Because the very core of our thinking is corrupted with the lie that we can find satisfaction for our souls apart from God, our beliefs about moral issues are likely to be wrong. This mental strategy to bypass God in our efforts to satisfy the thirst in our souls is brought out most clearly by the prophet Jeremiah. Read this passage carefully:

"Therefore I bring charges against you again," declares the Lord. "And I will bring charges against your children's children. Cross over to the coasts of Kittim and look, send to Kedar and observe closely; see if there has ever been anything like this: Has a nation ever changed its gods?

(Yet they are not gods at all.) But my people have exchanged their Glory for worthless idols. Be appalled at this, O heavens, and shudder with great horror,"declares the Lord. "My people have committed two sins: They have forsaken me, the spring of living water, and have dug their own cisterns, broken cisterns that cannot hold water." (Jer. 2:9–13)

Plainly a trial is in progress. God is bringing charges against His people. But why? The Almighty, speaking metaphorically, accuses them of preferring to dig their own broken cisterns rather than rely in humble dependence on the Lord for their life. How pained God must have felt as He observed His people spurning His offer of living water, free for the taking, and laboriously digging their own cisterns. (See illustration 5.)

Illustration 5

Matthew Henry said it well in his commentary on Jeremiah. The language is old-fashioned, but the point is powerful.

> When they came to quench their thirst there they found nothing but mud and mire and the filthy sediments of a standing lake. If we make an idol of anything – wealth or pleasure or honour – if we place our happiness in it, and promise ourselves the comfort and satisfaction in it which are to be had in God only, if we make it our joy and love, our hope and confidence we shall find it a cistern, which we take a great deal of pains to hew out and fill, and at the best, it will hold but a little water and that dead and flat. ... It is a broken cistern, that cracks and cleaves in hot weather so that the water is lost when we have most need of it. Let us therefore with purpose of heart cleave to the Lord only, for whither else shall we go? He has the words of eternal life.

There is something in all of us that hates the fact that apart from God we will never be able to satisfy the deep thirst and deep longings in our souls. Facing that truth requires that we adopt the position of helplessness – giving up our vain attempts to make life work without God – and helplessness is something our carnal nature abhors. We much prefer to be in control of the water we drink. And that is a strategy the Bible regards as foolish.

Perhaps an illustration will throw some more light on the point I am making. When I was twelve, in my native country of Wales, my class was instructed to write an essay on the theme of "War and Peace". After the task had been completed and the essays had been marked, the teacher stood at the front of the class and said something like this: "The essays have all been very good, but one is outstanding. That is the one written by Selwyn Hughes." I remember thinking to myself, *This feels so good to be singled out like this.*

Now picture me there as a boy of twelve. What do you know about me? Very little perhaps, but you know this: I was thirsty. My soul ached for something that no one or nothing had been able to satisfy. Now I was being singled out for praise in such a way that was like a drink to my parched soul. I liked what I felt and a strategy began to develop in my thinking that ran along this line: I can put words together in such a way that brings recognition and praise. Perhaps that's the route to life. Perhaps that will satisfy my thirst.

Of course, it wasn't as clear to me then, as I am putting it now, but something of that thinking began to develop in my mind, and although I studied to become an engineer, nothing satisfied me as much as putting words together on paper.

When later I was called to the Christian ministry, one of the first things I did was to enrol in a writing course. Later I began to write a daily devotional, which I called *Every Day with Jesus,* that is now read on a daily basis by close to half a million people in more than 120 countries around the world. Sometimes on my speaking engagements I am introduced as "the pastor with the world's largest daily congregation".

My success at writing has done two things for me. It has provided me a great deal of personal satisfaction, and it has given me a constant challenge to determine where my life is found – in writing or in God.

Several years ago one of my students sat in my office and said to me: "You talk to us a lot about finding our security and our significance in God. I wondered how you would feel if for some reason you were unable to write." I felt an inner tremble as I tried to reply. "Please leave me," I finally said. "I must deal with my heart quietly before God." In the hours that followed, I saw clearly that the strategy that had entered my mind as a boy of twelve was still there, covered over now by a veneer of spirituality but still very much part of my thinking.

Was I wrong in enjoying the fact that I am read by half a million people every day? Of course not. What was wrong was depending on that for life. I was drinking from a leaky cistern. I saw myself as a consummate professional rather than a desperately needy servant dependent on God alone for my soul's satisfaction. There and then I confessed my sin of misplaced dependency to the Lord, received His forgiveness, and rose to a new sense of commission.

The student's question is now never far from my mind when I write. Daily I kneel before God and say: "Lord, help me to draw always from You the water I need for my soul. Nothing satisfies but You, and You alone."

We now have three of the five points we need to understand the rise and development of problems. They can arise first because of some physical malfunction. They can arise, too, because our deep thirsts for God set up longings in our hearts that we try to satisfy outside of God. And because we are foolish thinkers, we try to quench our spiritual thirst by drinking from cisterns of our own making. These cisterns do not hold satisfying water. They also leak. We go from one broken cistern to another, driven by strategies that make us feel we are in control. How foolish.

The third key then to understanding how problems arise is – unnoticed wrong thinking.

OUR FREEDOM TO CHOOSE

The fourth component of the personality that must be brought into focus if we are to comprehend fully how problems arise is the will. Volitional causes can affect behaviour.

Several things need to be understood about the will and its function. As we have seen, God is a choosing being, and He made us with the power of choice also. Every one of us, every day of our lives, makes hundreds of choices. We get up in the morning and choose the clothes we will wear today. We choose what we will eat for breakfast. We choose what we listen to on the radio as we drive to work. We choose what we will have for lunch and what we will do after work.

The writer of the book of Proverbs reminds us that the Almighty makes choices too.

Many are the plans in a man's heart, but it is the Lord's purpose that prevails. (Prov. 19:21)

We make plans, and God makes plans, but He allows us to go with His plans or against them, though ultimately His plans will prevail. While we are free to choose, we are not free to choose the consequences of our choosing. Moses, when laying before the ancient Israelites the challenges they would face when entering into the promised land, said:

This day I call heaven and earth as witnesses against you that I have set before you life and death, blessings and curses. Now choose life, so that you and your children may live. (Deut. 30:19)

The fact that the great Creator has endowed us with the ability to go against His will, if we so choose, is perhaps one of the most amazing things about our construction as human beings. Read this passage taken from the prophecy of Isaiah:

How you have fallen from heaven, O morning star, son of the dawn! You have been cast down to the earth, you who once laid low the nations! You said in your heart, "I will ascend to heaven; I will raise my throne above the stars of God; I will sit enthroned on the mount of assembly, on the utmost heights of the sacred mountain. I will ascend above the tops of the clouds; I will make myself like the Most High." (Isa. 14:12–14)

Some commentators believe that here Isaiah is giving a description of the fall of Satan, and though that may be so, first and foremost he is talking about the king of Babylon. Cynddylan Jones, a famous Welsh preacher of a bygone generation, when referring to this text, makes the interesting point that five times in the passage we read the phrase "I will". "That," he points out, "is what sin is essentially – a created will going against the will of the Creator." He adds this comment: "How awesome that God would create a will that has the potential of competing with his will." How awesome indeed!

Also, the will does not have unlimited freedom. As someone put it: "We are not free to shout 'Fire' in a crowded room" (when there is no fire, of course). Someone else said, "My freedom to swing my arm ends at the tip of your nose." A person is free to jump off a high building; but having jumped, gravity takes over. We are free to act in many different ways, but our freedom is limited by law – either divine law or human law.

Because we are volitional beings, everything we do has a purpose. Often we are not conscious of the purpose behind our choices. I once spent time counselling a university student who kept failing his examinations even though he had an IQ of 150. It was not until I thoroughly came to understand his experiences as a child that I began to comprehend what purpose his behaviour served.

When he was a child, his parents used to say: "If you do not pass all your examinations, we will not love you." Growing up in this atmosphere of conditional love, he became an angry young man; but because his relationship with his parents did not allow him to express his angry feelings directly, he expressed them indirectly.

Here's another illuminating quotation from the book of Proverbs:

The purposes of a man's heart are deep waters, but a man of understanding draws them out. (Prov. 20:5)

The psychologist, Adler, made the point that the best way to understand any unit of behaviour is to ask yourself: What is the goal to which the behaviour is directed? What was the goal behind the university student's behaviour? It was retaliation. He wanted to get back at his parents in a way that did not involve expressing his anger directly. Only when he understood the goal behind his behaviour was he able to initiate change.

One of the most helpful insights I have ever discovered in my counselling ministry is that all behaviour moves towards a goal. (See illustration 6.) For years I spent a lot of time digging into people's pasts in order to find an explanation for their behaviour. Though that is an important part of understanding why people behave as they do, it is more important to comprehend the goal to which the behaviour is directed. Even the most bizarre behaviour, like a young girl risking death by anorexia nervosa – the determination to be thin – makes sense when the underlying purpose is understood.

Illustration 6

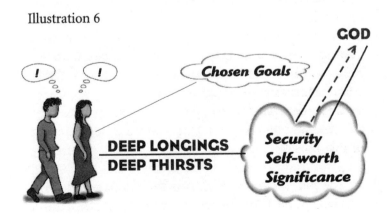

A further fact about the will is this: often we choose without realising we are choosing. The young university student I referred to earlier was choosing (albeit unconsciously) to fail his examinations, yet until the purpose behind his choice was exposed, he was not aware that he was choosing. But he was choosing nevertheless.

Hosea 7:8–9 says:

Ephraim mixes with the nations ... Foreigners sap his strength, but he does not realise it. His hair is sprinkled with grey, but he does not notice.

Most of us laugh at the idea of someone who has grey hair but doesn't notice it. But this is no different from a person who makes choices and doesn't realise it.

Larry Crabb has a powerful phrase that illuminates this concept of unrealised choices. "The loss of felt choice," he says, "does not mean the loss of real choice." One reason for this "unconscious choosing" is because many of our ideas about life are formed in our developmental years. And sometimes in the midst of trauma and disappointment and to anaesthetise the pain, we block out any conscious recollection of these events. But often when we are choosing in later life, not only are these past events kept out of consciousness, but the ideas and strategies that were formed from them are kept at bay too. They are hidden beneath the surface.

If you want to think more deeply about this, take an area of your life over which you feel you have little or no control – loss of temper, overeating or habitual masturbation, for example. You may feel you are driven by internal dynamics, driven against your will, but the truth is you are choosing to behave the way you do. Finding out what is behind those choices may require the help of a counsellor, but never forget, "The loss of felt choice does not mean the loss of real choice."

Remember, too, that the will does not function in a vacuum. Behind our will is our whole nature. Driven by a desire to find what our heart truly longs for – fulfilment – and prone to rely on ourselves to achieve that fulfilment more than on God, our mind develops strategies that quickly translate into a goal. If deep down in my heart I believe that amassing money is the route to happiness, then it will not be long before my mind will come up with ideas to achieve that goal, and from there the will takes over and presses on to what it believes is the goal to happiness.

Behind most problems is an unrecognised wrong goal. And most of the work in counselling is helping a person discover that goal.

The fourth key, therefore, to understanding how problems arise is unrecognised wrong goals.

HOW THE EMOTIONS AFFECT OUR BEHAVIOUR

One more consideration will complete our model. Our behaviour can have emotional causes. We are not just physical, relational, rational and volitional beings; we are emotional beings also – beings who can feel. One of the great debates in counselling literature takes place over the issue of how emotions arise and what are the most debilitating of these emotions.

The word *emotion* is derived from the Latin *emovare*, meaning "to move". Twelve fundamental emotions have been identified by psychologists and philosophers, and these are repeatedly mentioned in philosophical literature. They are divided into nine unpleasant emotions and three pleasant ones. The unpleasant ones are sorrow, fear, anger, jealousy, shame, disgust, pain, confusion and emptiness. The pleasant ones are love, joy and awe.

I have found it more helpful myself to categorise unpleasant or problem emotions into three main categories: first, emotions like anger, irritation, resentment, frustration and contempt; second, emotions such as fear, anxiety, worry, apprehension, pressure and forms of stress; third, emotions like guilt, shame, embarrassment and self-pity.

The interesting thing about these three streams of problem emotions is that most often they arise from a failure to reach the foolish goals we pursue. In other words, whenever any of the emotions I have mentioned arise within us, unless they are caused by physical malfunctioning, they are usually the result of some obstacle on the road to our goal – the goal we believe we have got to get to in order to experience personal happiness or fulfilment.

Our emotions, it is often pointed out, act like the red light on the dashboard of our car. The red light is not the problem but indicates a problem is occurring that needs attention. It is the same with negative emotions; their occurrence is a warning, telling us that all is not well in our internal emotional system.

"SIGNAL EMOTIONS"

I like the way Kevin Huggins puts it in *Parenting Adolescents:*

> God has given each of us a "warning system," to alert us when we are pursuing a foolish goal. This system consists of a series of "signal emotions" that reliably indicate the nature of the goal we are pursuing at any given moment. For example, the Apostle Paul admonished his readers to recognize their anger as a signal to alert them to potentially sinful attitudes and actions.

In order to understand how each of the three streams of emotions develops, it is necessary to identify the obstacles that lead to the rise of these negative feelings.

OBSTACLE 1

Feelings such as anger, irritation, resentment and contempt arise when a goal we have been pursuing is blocked by someone or some external circumstance. An illustration drawn from my counselling experience might help illuminate this point.

A middle-aged man, a believer, asked to see me because his doctor had diagnosed his physical problems as psychosomatic. During the initial interviews I learned that he was a handyman who liked to buy run-down property, refurbish it, then sell it for a much higher price than he paid for it. He had done this on three occasions in the past three years, and his wife, who was indulgent at first, got tired of living on a permanent building site and had informed him that unless he changed his ways and settled down in one home, she would leave him and consider their marriage to be over.

It was clear to me that although he did not appear to show anger on the surface, inwardly he was deeply hostile towards his wife. It took him a while to admit his anger – several sessions in fact. One day after he did, I said, "Finish this sentence for me: 'For me to live is ...'" He paused for a moment and said, "For me to live is ... possessing the most magnificent home in the community so that friends and relatives can visit us and be impressed with the way I achieved it." Then he added: "As I am not able to purchase one at this stage in my life, I am working to get there stage by stage, refurbishing a run-down place, then selling it, investing the profit and doing the same thing over and over again until one day I can afford to buy outright the house I want. What's wrong with that?"

"There's nothing wrong in desiring to live in a magnificent home," I said, "but I wonder if that desire has become such a demand inside you that you perceive it to be the route to your personal significance. The apostle Paul, in Philippians 1:21, said, 'For to me, to live is Christ and to die is gain.' I wonder if the desire to live in a magnificent home has turned into a demand, and you pursue that route because you see in that an offer of life. Is there a 'functional god' for you in what you are doing?"

I shared with him more about the concept of goal-oriented behaviour. I told him that when we foolishly take a certain course of action because we depend on that for our significance, rather than Christ, then, when that goal is blocked or undermined, frustration can erupt in feelings of irritation, anger and resentment.

"Here's my analysis of the situation," I said to him: "You have made it a goal one day to purchase the most magnificent home in your community because you perceive that it would offer you significance. Such a route is not necessary to those who already realise they are significant in Christ. Lacking this sense of identity, you pursue the goal with passion; and now that your wife threatens to leave you if you continue, the block to your goal has given rise to resentment, which in turn is the basis of your psychosomatic ailments." (See illustration 7.)

Illustration 7

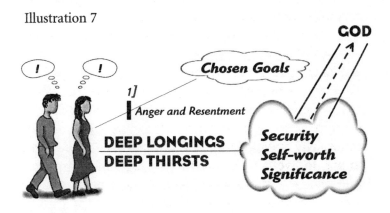

Further sessions involved exploring his wrong basic assumptions about life. As he came to learn that his relationship with God was sufficient to meet the deep longings of his heart to be seen as worthwhile, he abandoned his wrong goal, asked his wife's forgiveness, and within days the psychosomatic problems disappeared.

The irritation we feel is commensurate with how important and how dependent we are on the goal to achieve our worth. If we are only moderately dependent, then we feel the emotion only moderately; if we are strongly dependent, then we will feel the emotion strongly.

Feelings of anger, irritation, resentment and contempt for others arise because of an undermined goal. Something has intervened between us and the goal we foolishly believe will bring us the longings of our heart.

I know of no better scripture to pull this into focus than the one found in the epistle of James:

> What causes fights and quarrels among you? Don't they come from your desires that battle within you? You want something but don't get it. You kill and covet, but you cannot have what you want. You quarrel and fight. You do not have, because you do not ask God. (James 4:1–2)

OBSTACLE 2

Feelings of fear, anxiety, worry, pressure and the feelings that come from stress usually indicate a foolish goal whose attainment seems uncertain. These feelings often signal that the person has put his or her trust in something or someone for fulfilment but is unsure and uncertain that the objective will be realised.

Larry Crabb, in *Effective Biblical Counseling*, states that a strong contributing dynamic to this is a fear of failure. A person who fears that he or she may not reach the goal – a goal which may be perfectly attainable – will often waiver in anxious indecision.

> A husband desires a good marital relationship. He believes it is possible. His wife is willing and cooperative. But he still hesitates, suspended in a state of motionless indecision. Why? He is afraid that he might make a mess of things, that his best efforts would be substandard, so he does nothing. The premise on which he is operating is simple: if I try and fail, I will have to admit I'm a failure, and my self concept couldn't stand that. If I never try I can avoid failure.

Every one of us has to recognise that we can never guarantee every effort we make will bring us the success we desire, but never trying is sure to guarantee failure. Many choose the option of not trying because they prefer that to coming face-to-face with failure.

A woman I know was seriously ill when she was a child and, therefore, lacked a good and well-rounded education. She decided in her adult life to enrol in a one-year course to further her education. As she neared the end of the course and examinations, she dropped out, giving as the reason that her domestic problems were putting too much stress on her. Her instructor was confident she had sufficient grasp of the course "to fly through every one of the examination papers". She enrolled for the same course the following year, and once again, as she came towards the end of the course and the examinations loomed, she dropped out for the same reason – domestic problems.

Before enrolling for the third year, she decided to visit a counsellor who recognised immediately that she was struggling with a fear of failure and an uncertain goal. He asked her a searching question that took them to the heart of her problem: "What do you think would happen if you took the examination and failed?"

"I would be devastated," was her reply. From there the counsellor was able to proceed and show her how her uncertain goal arose from a fear that if she failed, her self-concept would not be able to stand it. "Your god is too small," said the counsellor. "If your confidence about who you are as a person rested in the true God and His evaluation of your worth, you would be able to take the examination, knowing that if you failed you would be disappointed but not devastated."

A radical reassessment of her basic assumptions about her worth took place. As she learned to put her trust in God and rely on Him and Him only for her sense of worth, she enrolled for the third time in the course, took the examinations, and came through with flying colours.

The basic emotional experience one feels when a goal is reachable but uncertain are feelings of anxiety and fear. (See illustration 8.)

Illustration 8

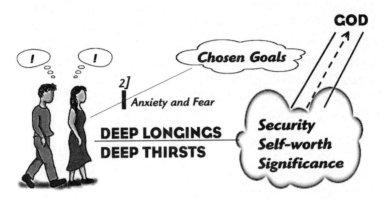

Many young men have been prevented from asking a girl out on a date because they fear being turned down. Such a young man may decide in his mind to do it, but then as he prepares to follow through on his decision, he wonders how he will feel if she turns him down. His desire for the date can be strong and solid, but as he reaches for the phone or prepares to approach her, a fear of failure can arise in his heart that is stronger than his desire. The block is not outside him but inside him.

If he perceives that reaching the goal of a successful date is where his identity as a person lies, he can withdraw from pursuing that goal by his fear of failure. He may stand by the telephone for several minutes, even pick up the handset, press a few digits, then hang up. Some have confessed to doing this a dozen times.

OBSTACLE 3

The third stream of problem emotions are those that arise from pursuing a goal that is unattainable. Guilt, shame and self-pity are some of the emotions that appear in this category.

When we hold within ourselves the perception that attaining a certain goal carries the promise that there life is to be found, failure to reach it can result in feelings such as guilt and shame. Some goals, which people set for themselves, are unattainable, no matter how hard they try. (See illustration 9.)

One woman I worked with, a missionary, told me that she was continually plagued with feelings of guilt and shame, despite the fact she was not involved in any moral violations. During the course of counselling, it became clear that she strongly believed that she must do everything perfectly. "Every night," she said, "when I am on the mission field, I make a list of the things I have to

Illustration 9

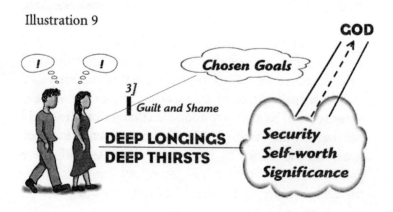

do the next day; and if I am not able to do them all, I go to my bed at night with great feelings, guilt, embarrassment and shame."

This woman came to believe that good feelings about herself depended on doing everything perfectly. Her objective was the unattainable goal of perfection. Whenever she failed to achieve her goal, she came down hard on herself with words of self-derogation, invective and despairing remorse. Her problem was resolved when she changed the basis of her beliefs and came to understand that good feelings about herself depended not on doing everything perfectly but on how well she related to God and lived in the light of His evaluation of her worth.

The fifth key then to understanding what lies behind our problems is unsettling negative emotions.

We are ready now to complete our thinking in relation to how problems arise in the personality. We began by making the point that before we can overcome our problems we must first understand how they arise and how they are maintained.

The source can be physical – a malfunction in the body that carries over to the soul. If there is no physical basis for the problem, then it usually arises and develops because of a deep sense of unfulfilment caused by a failure to let God be God. Based on the fact that we are thirsty people, we will seek ways to find satisfaction for our souls, and whatever we believe will bring us that satisfaction will become a goal. We experience any interference to those goals in the form of negative emotions. And these emotions, depending on how important the goals are to us, can be deeply debilitating and incapacitating.

Here then in summarised form are the five causes behind our personal problems:

- Uncorrected physical disorders
- Unsatisfied deep longings
- Unnoticed wrong thinking
- Unrecognised wrong goals
- Unsettling negative emotions

At this point you may be saying to yourself: *I know how to correct physical problems – get good medical attention – but how do I go about dealing with the other four areas?* That will come later. First, as I have pointed out, it is important to understand ourselves better so that we can bring all parts of our personality into submission to Christ and thus experience the thrill of Christ empowered living. Before we move on to look at the principles for overcoming our problems, we have one more issue to confront – the danger of trying to live life without depending on God. To that issue we now turn.

Chapter 8

LIVING DANGEROUSLY

Now and again there arises in the Christian Church a man or woman with a message that makes us sit up and think. Such a man is Charles Colson, the one-time assistant to President Richard Nixon. No doubt you know the story of how he went from the White House to a prison cell because of his involvement in the Watergate scandal. Since his conversion to Jesus Christ, he has shown himself to have a clear grasp of Christian truths and principles and has a unique way of presenting them. Many regard him as one of today's most articulate prophets in the Christian Church. He speaks directly and to the point. Colson doesn't mince his words.

In his book *Loving God*, he writes with great lucidity and logic about some of the issues facing Christians in a postmodern society. "There seems to be a desire in many of today's Christians," he says, "to be more interested in finding themselves than in finding God."

He writes:

> This not so magnificent obsession to "find ourselves" has spawned a whole new set of counterfeit values: we worship fame, success, materialism and celebrity. We want to "live for success" as we "look out for number one" and we don't mind winning through intimidation. ... And in the midst of all this we have the church – those who follow Christ. For the church, this ought to be an hour of opportunity. The church alone can provide a moral vision to a wandering people, the church alone can step into the vacuum and demonstrate the truth that there is a sovereign living God who is the source of truth. But the church is almost in as much trouble as the culture for the church has bought into the same value system; fame, success, materialism and celebrity. Preoccupation with those values has also perverted the church's message. ...
>
> A popular daily devotional quotes Psalm 65:9 "The streams of God are filled with water" and paraphrases it: "I fill my mind to overflowing with thoughts of prosperity and success. I affirm that God is my source and God is unlimited." This is not just religious adaptation of the look out for number one, winner take all, God helps those who help themselves gospel of our culture; it is heresy.

How deeply distressing it is that so many in contemporary Christian society – people who should know better – get caught up in pursuing lesser goals than God and His glory. Many of the things we pursue in life are legitimate objectives (education, excellence, physical prowess, etc.), but when these objectives become a goal that we believe we have to reach in order to maintain a sense of personal intactness, we are misplacing our dependency. Unless God and His glory are the overriding goals in our lives, then we live dangerously.

A POWERFUL
PROPHETIC INDICTMENT

Step with me into the time tunnel and go back to some words written by an ancient prophet by the name of Amos. Here's a thumbnail biographical sketch of this man.

Amos ministered in Israel about 750 BC and lived in a small town called Tekoa, south of Bethlehem. He carried a great burden for his people, or as one commentary put it: "His people were his great burden."

Amos was a layperson who disclaimed professional status as a prophet:

"I am no prophet, nor a prophet's son; but I am a herdsman, and a dresser of sycamore trees, and the Lord took me from following the flock, and the Lord said to me, 'Go, prophesy to my people Israel.'"
(Amos 7:14–15, RSV)

The *Holman Bible Dictionary* says about him: "Because of God's call, Amos assumed his prophetic responsibilities as a lonely voice prophesying from both the desert and the villages. He indicted both Judah and Israel, challenging the superficial qualities of religious institutions. For Amos, his call and his continuing ministry rested in God's initiative and in his sustaining power: 'The lion has roared; who will not fear? The Lord God has spoken; who can but prophesy?'" (3:8, RSV).

At the time Amos prophesied, Israelite society was in a state of spiritual decay, and corruption was rampant. The rich exploited the poor and justice was distorted. He was especially troubled by what he saw happening in the north of the kingdom and, like Colson, lowered the boom on the people in these powerfully challenging words:

> *This is what the Sovereign Lord showed me: a basket of ripe fruit. "What do you see, Amos?" he asked. "A basket of ripe fruit," I answered. Then the Lord said to me, "The time is ripe for my people Israel; I will spare them no longer."* (Amos 8:1–2)

The basket of ripe summer fruit was a Hebrew word picture that indicated Israel was ripe for judgment. They were in a desperate spiritual condition and were ripe for divine retribution.

Read on and see why God was so incensed with them:

> *Hear this, you who trample the needy and do away with the poor of the land, saying, "When will the New Moon*

*be over that we may sell grain, and the Sabbath be
ended that we may market wheat?" – skimping the
measure, boosting the price and cheating with dishonest
scales, buying the poor with silver and the needy for a
pair of sandals, selling even the sweepings with the
wheat.* (Amos 8:4–6)

The thing that riled God was the fact that people went
to the temple on the Sabbath, paid lip service to God in
prayer and worship, but that was not really where their
hearts were focused. They couldn't wait for the Sabbath
to be over so they could get back to the marketplace and
fill the emptiness in their souls with the buzz they got
from dishonest and manipulative practices – skimping
on the measures, jacking up the price and mixing
sweepings with the wheat.

Life for them was defined not by their relationship
with God but by their ability to manipulate and exploit
others. Their souls came alive, not in the temple but in
the marketplace. Do you see a parallel between Amos'
time and ours? I most certainly do. Our modern-day
churches have within them many people like this. They
go to church on Sunday, appear to enter into worship,
but deep down in their hearts they can't wait for Monday
to come around so that they can get back to the
workplace (make a killing on the stock exchange?), and
throw themselves into activity that brings a sense of
passion and aliveness in their souls that is not there when
they stand in the presence of God.

How did they get this way? Largely because their
priests and teachers failed them. Another prophet by the

name of Jeremiah challenged the priests of his day because they did not expose the self-centred patterns of the people, and likened the priest's superficial approach to the people's lack of spirituality to putting a plaster on a wound that requires more expert attention.

Here's how he put it:

They dress the wound of my people as though it were not serious. "Peace, peace," they say, when there is no peace. Are they ashamed of their loathsome conduct? No, they have no shame at all; they do not even know how to blush. (Jer. 6:14–15)

I am not a prophet nor the son of a prophet, but I believe the biggest indictment against the contemporary Christian Church is that so many pastors and teachers fail to make clear the design of God in the personality and to remind God's people that if we do not satisfy our thirst in Him, then we will be powerfully drawn to looking elsewhere to have our thirst quenched. We simply can't go through life thirsty. We have to get it quenched – if not with God, then with something else. Pastors and teachers who try to help people in their Christian walk without making this issue clear are "dressing people's wounds as if they were not serious".

I have come to the conclusion that this is the issue underlying most spiritual problems.

Larry Crabb spells it out in these three terse propositions:

- Everyone is thirsty.
- Everyone longs and seeks to have their thirst satisfied.
- Any attempt to satisfy that thirst outside of a relationship with Jesus Christ will lead to problems.

Can anything be simpler? If we do not find our satisfaction in God, we will find it elsewhere and in ways that violate the design of our beings.

Listen now to what the prophet Amos says will be the end of those who go to the temple on the Sabbath, engage in superficial worship, then go out to meet the needs of their souls in ways that dishonour the Lord:

"The days are coming," declares the Sovereign Lord, "when I will send a famine through the land – not a famine of food or a thirst for water, but a famine of hearing the words of the Lord." (8:11)

Follow me closely now because this was a serious issue for Israel, and it's also a serious issue for us. God was saying to Israel: If you do not pay attention to the need of your soul to maintain a close relationship with Me, a time will come when you won't be able to hear My words, and I will leave you to your own devices. In other words, if you don't *heed* My Word, then you won't *hear* My Word.

SPIRITUAL DEAFNESS

I often wonder, as I mingle with Christians in church, how many of them really are quenching their deep longings and thirst in God. On the surface it appears that in many cases they are; they sing lustily, raise their hands in worship, some even dance in church. But how many understand that life is not found in a church, but in God? Unless we draw our life from Him, not only on Sunday but every day of the week, we will be quickly drawn to other sources of satisfaction.

We live dangerously if we do not understand and make God supreme. And if we continue in this way – paying lip service to the fact that Christ is our life yet not fully depending on Him – then maybe we will end up with that most serious of religious conditions, spiritual deafness.

In order to make clear the danger we are in when we do not continually depend on God for our life and seek to quench our spiritual thirst in Him, I must add a few more components to the basic theory I presented in the two previous chapters. But before I do, permit a brief summary:

God has designed us as *relational* beings who are meant first to relate to Him and then to others. The closer we relate to Him and draw from His resources, the more equipped we are to relate well to others and cope with whatever life brings. We are also *thinking* beings who, because of the Fall, have a tendency to believe incorrectly about where life is found.

Whatever we believe will bring us the satisfaction our hearts long for quickly translates into a goal, and because we are *choosing* beings, we pursue goals that we erroneously believe will provide for us spiritually and psychologically. But depending on any goal that is less than God leaves us vulnerable to other sources of satisfaction. When something happens to undermine our goals, or they are uncertain or unreachable, because we are emotional beings, we will also experience problem emotions. The strength of those emotions depends in varying degrees on how we perceive those goals as being important to our personal intactness. (See illustration 10.)

Illustration 10

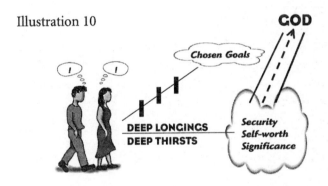

Multitudes of Christians are in the position where they draw their life and strength not so much from God but from their dependency on a goal they believe they need to reach in order to make their lives work. And many have sufficient ego strength to keep going for years – paying lip service to God and Christian things but drawing more on natural energy than spiritual power to support them in their journey through life.

Some, however, whenever their goal is blocked, experience varying degrees of anger or resentment, but they are not incapacitated by these feelings because they have within them sufficient ego strength to overcome the obstacle and press on towards their goal. The same is true of people who experience a block to their goal in the form of uncertainty; they draw from within themselves enough energy to press on to their goal notwithstanding the anxiety or fear that arises within them.

Then there are those who, when faced with an unreachable goal, will, despite the problem emotions of guilt and shame, draw on their natural energy because their ego strength keeps them moving towards their goal.

People who continue to live this way, striving towards goals they erroneously believe will give them life and overcoming all the obstacles by sheer force of their own inner energy and strength, are extremely vulnerable to serious personal problems. One psychologist describes such people as preneurotic in the sense that, although they do not presently experience neurotic problems (excessive and debilitating emotions), they are candidates for such problems and can quickly tip over into neuroticism at any given moment.

Perhaps here I should define *neurosis*. The term *neurosis* refers to a disorder of thinking, feeling or behaving characterised by a loss of joy in living and an overuse of defence mechanisms. A neurotic person can be compared to a drug addict. Each is likely to experience emotional pain. The addict uses chemicals to escape pain; the neurotic uses defence mechanisms as a means of escape. Each accepts some pain to avoid a greater pain

– the legitimate suffering designed to find freedom. The chemical addict lives with the physical pain to avoid the pain of inner turmoil. Neurosis is always a substitute for legitimate suffering.

Psychologist Larry Crabb put it this way in *Effective Biblical Counseling*:

> I think of guilt, anxiety and resentment as preneurotic experiences. Full-fledged neurosis occurs when a person develops a symptom or symptom pattern designed to avoid further insult to his self esteem. The goal of the prenuerotic is to overcome the obstacle and to reach his fervently desired goal (changed wife, live perfectly, make money, etc.). He willingly will evaluate the effectiveness of his goal oriented behavior and adopt new strategies which hold promise of crossing the barrier and reaching the goal.

Hundreds of thousands of Christians all over the world are living less than an abundant life. They could be described as being in the preneurotic stage. Their condition is not bad enough for counselling but not good enough to be called "abundant living" either. They go through life either angry at what happens to them, living with feelings of guilt and self-derogation, or they spend their days tense and anxious or fearful. They are not able to say with Hosea: "The joy of the Lord is my strength."

At some point – and no one can predict the moment – the frustration of living under such strain can precipitate debilitating emotional problems. This happens when the person stops trying to overcome the blocks to his or her goal and seeks a less painful and frustrating existence. The triggers can be anything – a family row, a snub, a redundancy, being overlooked for promotion, a child's failing an examination or a financial loss. In the case of one man I knew, it happened when he reached his fiftieth birthday.

Here's the story. Prior to John's (not his real name) reaching his fiftieth birthday, I sent him a birthday card affirming our friendship over many years. A few days later he telephoned me to thank me for the card and in conversation let drop that the day after his birthday he had plunged into a state of deep depression. He told me also that he had consulted his doctor, who had diagnosed his depression as exogenous (a medical term indicating it was not due to chemical disturbances in the body), and he asked for my help in counselling.

The next day we met and talked. John had aspired, almost from the day of his conversion, to become a minister of the gospel. He attended a Bible college, and although he became a fairly good preacher, no church to which he had applied thought him suitable to be their pastor. His efforts to find a pastoral role went on for years, but instead of accepting the fact that this clearly was not God's direction for his life, he continued to pursue it as a goal. (Keep in mind that whenever I use the word *goal*, it has the special meaning of an objective we pursue because we believe the achievement is where life is to be found.)

As we talked, it became clear that for years his thinking and self-talk had proceeded along this line: "In order to be secure, worthwhile and significant, I need to be accepted into full-time Christian ministry." This, of course, was not true. In order for the deep longings of his heart to be satisfied and to experience himself as secure, worthwhile and significant, he needed nothing more than his relationship with Jesus Christ.

The frustration he experienced over the decades in not achieving his goal was overcome by his steadfast determination to pursue his goal in the hope that one day it would be realised. However, the thought began to surface in his mind that having tried unsuccessfully to reach his goal, now at fifty years of age there was little likelihood of his ever reaching it. The pain of this realisation was so great that unconsciously he began to look for a way to avoid those painful feelings. And at this point he moved from being preneurotic to neurotic.

THE ROUTE TO SAFETY

Most neurotic symptoms have a functional significance in that they can give the person concerned an excuse for avoiding further frustration (I can't continue doing what I was doing because I am struggling with this neurotic condition) or provide the person with a dampening-down of painful existential feelings such as insecurity, insignificance or inferiority. In my friend's case, as long as he saw some hope of reaching the goal – becoming a minister – which he erroneously believed could bring him satisfaction and fulfilment in his soul, he was unlikely to become a candidate for exogenous depression. However, when he gave up hope of reaching the goal and he was faced with the painful feelings of insecurity, insignificance and inferiority, which had been kept at bay by his efforts to reach the goal, his unconscious helped him to cope with the debilitating emotions arising within him by directing him to the zone of safety. (See illustration 11.)

Illustration 11

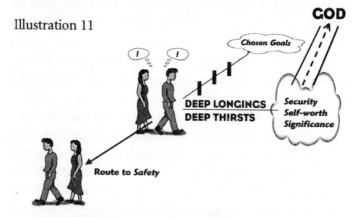

My friend's depression had a functional significance. It helped get him off the hook, so to speak. He moved from the preneurotic to the neurotic stage because, when he saw that he was unlikely to realise his goal, he sought to find relief from the sense of insecurity, insignificance and inferiority by moving to a position where increasing feelings of worthlessness were some-what dampened.

The depression provided the dampening effect his disturbed emotions needed. Rather than pursuing a goal unlikely to provide worth, he now directed his efforts to protecting whatever little feelings remain. He gave up the struggle to find worth through the hope of becoming a minister and moved into a holding pattern, the design of which was to protect whatever feelings of worth remain.

Freud was credited with the following statement (whether or not you agree with his psychology, his words make a lot of sense): "Neurosis is the exchange of one pain for another." Based on my own experience of dealing with people, I would add this: The pain of neurosis is a much easier pain to cope with and bear than the pain of feeling worthless, useless and purposeless.

Whenever I have told this story to students, those who have experienced depression usually object by saying, "How does depression do this?" There are, of course, many types of depression, and it can descend upon the personality in various forms. Some depression comes from chemical changes in the body. Some depression comes from loss of meaning. I have learned to respect the many causes of depression. But I am convinced that one form of depression acts to dampen the acute feelings of loss that come when a person faces a sense of loss of self-worth. It says in effect, "You will feel the pain of depression, but this pain is not as bad as the pain of worthlessness that would hit you with all its force if I were not here to dampen it."

The worst possible emotional feeling a person can experience is the feeling that one is unloved and has no point on being on the earth. That feeling is so devastating to the soul that it would tear it apart if there was not an unconscious mechanism designed to dampen those feelings and support the person through that trying period. Sometimes depression can be a defence against that devastation.

WHAT'S WORSE THAN DEPRESSION?

What is worse than depression? Feeling that no one loves you, no one cares for you, no one sees any point or purpose in your being around. And feeling that in all its intensity. For your soul to look into the universe and believe God doesn't seem to care about you, others don't care about you, and you don't care about you produces feelings that can be devastating. Unless the mechanism of depression dampens it, the soul will fall apart.

In my friend's case depression was a kindness, saying: "I will help support you until you regain a proper perspective. The feelings you get will be painful but not as painful as if I were not here."

My native country is Wales. My father worked in the coal mines. After my theological training in Bristol, England, I returned to Wales and spent a few years as a pastor in one of its mining communities. As soon as I arrived, I announced to my congregation that I would set apart one day a week for those who would like to talk with me about any problems they were experiencing.

One of my very first counselling appointments was a man who said he was unable to continue working in the mines because he had developed a fear of entering the cage that transported miners down into the depths of the earth. I discovered in the initial interview that his fear of entering the cage had developed almost immediately after he had been promoted to a job he felt ill equipped to handle.

I did not at that stage of my life have the understanding I now have of how the personality functions, and I was unable to help him in the way I think I now could. Here's how I would do it if he were sitting before me today. Working from the hypothesis that neurotic symptoms are designed to reach the goal of safety, I would want to explore whether his newly developed fear of entering the cage was related to his feelings of inadequacy concerning his new job. Had something about his promotion produced a threat that deep down he wanted to avoid?

Today my theory would be something like this: Finding himself in a new position in which he desperately wanted to excel, his goal was success. However, lurking deep inside him was a fear that he might not come up to expectations – a fear of failure. This fear nagged at him constantly, creating a great deal of frustrating anxiety, which became an obstacle to his goal. I would want to explore his self-talk. Was he saying something like this perhaps: "I am not sure I can do this job, and if I fail, I will not be able to handle the loss to my self-worth."

At that time he was preneurotic. Had he come to me at that point, I would have been able to help him by encouraging him to change his assumptions about where his true worth as a person really lay – not in what he did (or failed to do) but in who he was in Christ. Once convinced of that, he would be able to admit to himself his lack of skills for the job or apply for further training. Whatever decision he made, he would have been held by the conviction that success or failure on the job did not determine his worth from God's perspective.

However, largely unaware of what was going on inside him, I believe he moved from the preneurotic stage to the neurotic when, in an attempt to find safety from the possible loss of self-worth through a failure to perform effectively at his new job, he unconsciously attached his fear of failure to fear of entering the cage. The consequence of this fear was that he had to inform his employers he could no longer work underground because he had developed, as he put it, "a strange fear that prevents me from going down into the bowels of the earth".

His employers arranged for him to have a less responsible position on the surface, and although his salary was just half of what he would have received in his newly promoted position underground, he rationalised that this had nothing to do with him but was one of the unfortunate consequences of his developing an irrational fear. The fear, though he did not realise it, was doing what the personality designed it to do – protect him from the loss of self-worth, a protection a child of God resting in the biblical understanding that we are "complete in Him" (Col. 2:10, NKJV) does not need. The solution to his problem lay in understanding that his worth from God's point of view did not depend on his performance. Once this was fully comprehended and given time to sink into the depths of his being, I would expect his irrational fear to vanish like a mist before the rising sun. He would likely be able to descend in the cage and return to his old job underground.

One of the interesting books of modern times is *The Peter Principle*. It talks about the fact that many people in industry have some form of breakdown when they are given a promotion they feel they cannot fulfil. It talks about promoting people "to the level of their incompetence". They might function well in middle management, but they break down when they are promoted to senior management. The problem is often rooted in a fear of failure.

It would be wrong to suggest that all neurotic symptoms, such as excessive guilt, fears and depression, are an attempt by the person to head for safety. Often they are psychosomatic symptoms of unhealthy emotional states. However, I have found that when these things occur, it is well worth exploring the possibility that they may be an attempt to head down the route to safety.

What has often amazed me is that people can be Bible teachers, preachers and evangelists, having what seems to be a good relationship with God, but they still allow their thinking to move toward the erroneous idea that their efforts bring them the sense of wholeness. I have known people to throw a tennis match because, rather than face possible failure and the consequent loss of self-worth that may bring, they console themselves that they gave the match to the other person rather than had it taken away from them. They had not lost the match; they had surrendered it.

Let's return to my friend who experienced sudden depression. What was his goal? To be a minister. What was the block to the goal? It was undermined by the idea that his increasing age would preclude him from ever being in charge of a church. And the consequent emotion? Undoubtedly it was anger. Then the repressed anger produced a form of depression, which dampened his increasing feelings of loss of self-worth.

What was my counsel? He was pursuing a wrong goal. There was nothing wrong with his aspiring to be a minister, but that was not where his dependency for his soul's satisfaction ought to be. He changed by an act of will, asked God's forgiveness for seeking to drink from a leaky well, and found a new goal in God. He re-established his priorities, and from then on all was different. The depression lifted within twenty-four hours, and to this day he enjoys ministering where and when he can. The last time I spoke to him he said, "If God wants to use me in the pulpit, fine; if not, that is fine also. My security is in Him, not in what I do."

The model I am describing can be presented like this: As long as a person reaches the goal he believes he needs to achieve security, significance and worth, he is unlikely to become a candidate for psychological problems. However, when he loses sight of that goal or gives up hope of reaching the goal, the unconscious can relieve the emotional pressure by depression.

Many people never reach their desired goal. They never experience satisfaction, but they never experience devastation either. They can hold themselves together. They are what some refer to as "miserable Christians", an oxymoron if ever there was one. Many people struggle with the feelings that come from blocked, unreachable or uncertain goals; but they are not incapacitated by these feelings and so have the emotional strength to avert deep emotional problems. Multitudes are living like this both inside and outside the Church. But here's the danger.

These people can easily become candidates for deeper emotional problems.

We live dangerously when we try to find worth in *what we do* rather than in *who we are*. Our identity must be in God. What are the keys to living in a way that will save us from being tipped over into neuroticism? That is what will occupy our attention in the second half of this book.

Chapter 9

GOD'S PERFECT MAN

Two preachers from Tennessee were talking about their pulpit and pastoral work. One had just embarked on a literary composition. "I am writing a small, one-dollar pamphlet to explain how evil came into the universe." With typical Tennessee wit, the other replied: "Better make it a two-dollar pamphlet and tell us how to get evil out of the universe."

That story introduces this second half of the book, which begins the constructive part of our thinking.

In the previous section we considered several thoughts:

- God designed humankind to reflect and mirror His own character and personality.

- Made in God's image, the first human pair functioned as microcosms of the Deity – relationally, rationally, volitionally and emotionally.

- God's image was intended to express itself through a physical body that would forever be the expression of the spirit.

- When Adam and Eve sinned, they distanced themselves from the Deity and alienated themselves from the life of God.

- From that time on no one has functioned in the way God originally designed.

- Problems develop when we fail to function in the way we were designed.

If ever this ruined instrument is to be put together again, it must be from without. There can be no reconstruction within the realm of destruction.

Divine Love was ready to hear the call for a Deliverer. As one poet put it:

> In the heart of man a cry;
> In the heart of God – supply.

How different this is from William Henley's poem *Invictus*, which reflects a stubborn stoicism, an attitude of defiance and a way of making it on one's own.

> Out of the night that covers me,
>   Black as the pit from pole to pole,
> I thank whatever Gods there be,
>   For my unconquerable soul.
> In the fell chance of circumstances,
>   I have not winced nor cried aloud,

Under the bludgeonings of chance,
  My head is bloody but unbowed.
It matters not how strait the gate,
  How charged with punishments the scroll,
I am the master of my fate,
  I am the captain of my soul.
                    —William Earnest Henley

Throughout the Old Testament – in fact ever since God promised that the seed of the woman would crush the serpent's head in Genesis 3:15 – God kept alive the fact that one day a Deliverer would come. In the first thirty-nine books of the Bible, it is as though a trumpeter takes his stand on the turrets of almost every book and announces the coming of the Saviour. "Get ready," every book seems to say: "Get ready; He is coming."

The pastor of the church in which I was brought up in my native Wales used to say that Christ can be seen in every book of the Old Testament. Then he would run through its thirty-nine books like this: In Genesis He is the seed of the woman; in Exodus, the Passover Lamb; in Leviticus, the prophet like unto Moses; in Numbers, the Pillar of Cloud by day and the Pillar of Fire by night; in Deuteronomy, the Smitten Rock, and so on. I heard him say on one occasion, "Looking for Jesus in the Old Testament is like looking for the name *Jones* in a telephone directory."

The ancient seers of God strained their eyes through the darkness of the future and caught the gleam of a coming Light. They knew something wonderful was impending in heaven. Isaiah spoke for all the prophets when, looking forward and predicting the coming of the Messiah, he cried:

The people walking in darkness have seen a great light. (Isa. 9:2)

Around two thousand years ago that "great Light" was seen on earth when God came and dwelt amongst us in the form of His Son. John, in his Gospel, put it like this:

The Word became flesh and made his dwelling among us. We have seen his glory, the glory of the One and Only, who came from the Father, full of grace and truth. (John 1:14)

"Christianity," it has been said, "is not just a religion of influences and values and principles. It is a religion of happenings, events, of plain historical occurrences." It belongs to the very marrow of the gospel that God came to this world in the person of His Son at a certain hour in history, lived in a certain place, died on a cross, was buried and came back from the dead, then ascended back to His Father, and one day will return to this world. The Christian faith has at its heart certain facts, and none is more wonderful than God's taking upon Himself human form.

At this point it is perhaps appropriate to ask: Was it necessary for Christ to become human? Flesh. The Chaldean soothsayers, summoned by Nebuchadnezzar to interpret his dream, found the idea incredible:

"What the king asks is too difficult. No-one can reveal it to the king except the gods, and they do not live among men." (Dan. 2:11)

Even King Solomon seemed to think it impossible that God could become man:

"But will God really dwell on earth? The heavens, even the highest heaven, cannot contain you. How much less this temple I have built!" (1 Kings 8:27)

DID GOD HAVE TO BECOME HUMAN?

We know that Christ came into this world; we attest that fact every time we write the date. But the question that has to be answered is why. What were the reasons prompting the Trinity to devise such a humiliating plan? "For Jesus to become a man and live as a man amongst men," said the great preacher C.H. Spurgeon, "meant more humiliation than for an angel to become a worm."

E. Stanley Jones, the famous missionary to India, posed this question in his book *The Word Became Flesh*, "Did God have to become human?" His answer is worth considering:

There are a number of ways God can reveal Himself. He can reveal Himself through nature. But not perfectly. I look up to God through Nature and come to the conclusion that God is Law. But the revelation is a very impersonal kind of law. Then God reveals Himself through prophets and teacher and sage but not perfectly, for the medium of revelation is imperfect and the message coming through that imperfect medium partakes of that imperfection. Then there is the method of revelation through a book. We must be grateful for every inspired word which has come down to us through a book – grateful but not satisfied. A book is impersonal and God is the infinitely personal. A book is the Word become word, not the Word become flesh.

What then do we need for a perfect revelation of God? A life must come among us – a Divine life. That has happened. A life came among us and lived publicly for thirty-three years. I look up through Jesus, the Son and know what God is like. He is a Christ like God, and if He is then He is a good God and trustable. I could think of nothing higher; I could be content with nothing less.

We said earlier that whatever we mean by that elusive word *personality*, the least it could mean is that we can relate, think, feel and choose. That is what constitutes the image of God in humankind. And nowhere did the image of God shine more clearly in human form than in the life and person of Jesus of Nazareth. And it is in Jesus that the great Triune God comes nearest to our understanding.

The expression "the image of God" never occurs in the Old Testament after the account of creation, except in Genesis 9. In the New Testament, however, it appears several times. In 1 Corinthians 11:7; 2 Corinthians 4:4; Colossians 1:15; Colossians 3:10; and Hebrews 1:3. In 1

Corinthians 11:7 the apostle Paul refers to humankind as the original divine intention and speaks of him as the "image and glory of God." In 2 Corinthians 4:4, he refers to Christ as the "image of God", and in Colossians 1:15 and Colossians 3:10, he declares that the original divine intention may be restored through Christ.

In Hebrews 1:3, Christ is referred to as reflecting God's image. The word used there is a much stronger one (not *eikon* but *kharakter*), which means an exact copy or engraving. Jesus Christ is infinitely more than a shadow of God; He is the effulgence of His glory and the image of His substance.

GOD'S PERFECT MAN

How perfectly did Christ display the image of God on earth? Look with me through many of the scriptures that help us see His perfect personality at work. Let's begin with His developing mind.

Little is said about our Lord's childhood. Although born in Bethlehem, He grew up in Nazareth. Quite literally our Lord put Nazareth on the map. It was not mentioned anywhere in Hebrew literature until it became associated with Him. It seems to have had something of a lowly reputation (John 1:46).

One theologian claimed that Jesus never really had a childhood. "He was grave, sad and preoccupied," he claimed. "He moved about with a weight upon him ... would never have looked young." Surely that is a caricature. I picture Him in his early years happily playing in the shavings on the carpentry floor, fetching timber for Joseph's trade, trying His hand with the carpentry tools.

And the child grew and became strong; he was filled with wisdom, and the grace of God was upon him. (Luke 2:40)

The only clear picture we have of His childhood is when He accompanied His parents to Jerusalem at the age of twelve. And here we have a window into His mind as He sits among the most erudite of the religious leaders asking them questions. Note how simply yet sublimely Luke describes Jesus' modesty and teachability:

Listening to them and asking them questions. (v.46)

Already He was beginning to realise His unique identity and destiny. Mary, His mother, expostulated with Him for getting lost and staying behind in Jerusalem. She said, "Son, why have you treated us like this? Your father and I have been anxiously searching for you" (v. 48). He responded:

Didn't you know I had to be in my Father's house? (v.49)

Note how Mary said, "your father", referring to Joseph. Jesus said "my Father", referring of course to Jehovah. Clearly at the age of twelve, He was beginning to comprehend the idea of His mission on the earth.

G. Campbell Morgan suggests there are three ways in which we might know God – creation, revelation and direct communication. All these avenues were open to Jesus, he says, and through them, by reason of His sinless mind, He saw all that was to be seen.

Creation, for example, would have been an open book to Him. In Him there was no clouding of intelligence. Revelation, the ancient scrolls containing God's Word, would have come alive with meaning, and in them and through them the voice of God would have resonated in His soul. He would have answered to that Voice with all the naturalness of a child in the immediate presence of his father. And His communication with God would have been immediate and uninterrupted. These things can be said about no one other than Jesus.

At about thirty years of age, He left Nazareth to become an itinerant preacher, but after a few months, He returned and visited the synagogue on the Sabbath day. He spoke to the congregation, and as they listened to Him, they were astonished at His words. Someone asked, "What's this wisdom that has been given Him? Isn't this the carpenter?" And when in Jerusalem He spoke in the temple courts, the Jews were amazed and said about Him, "How did this man get such learning without having studied?" (John 7:15).

Notice how Jesus answered that question: "My teaching is not my own. It comes from him who sent me" (v.16).

He continued, "If anyone chooses to do God's will, he will find out whether my teaching comes from God or whether I speak on my own" (v.17). The one who does the will of God perfectly is the one who understands all mysteries. He never learned, for He had no need to learn. Learning is a process made necessary because of the Fall. Prior to the Fall, and without the need for learning, Adam could name all the animals. The psalmist put it this way:

> The Lord confides in those who fear him; he makes his covenant known to them. (Psa. 25:14)

The one who perfectly does the will of God is the one who understands all mysteries and is familiar with things that those who disobey His will can never comprehend. To quote G. Campbell Morgan again:

> The secrets that lie hidden in Nature, fallen man with clouded intelligence must search after, but God's unfallen Man will read them upon the open page of Nature, discovering immediately the deepest philosophies of life.

Our Lord was perfect in His mental make-up.

OUR LORD'S EMOTIONAL MAKE-UP

Our Lord was perfect also in His emotional nature. His mind, seeing God perfectly, loved Him supremely. An unclouded intelligence will always result in a perfect consciousness of God. As our Lord Himself put it:

> Blessed are the pure in heart, for they will see God. (Matt. 5:8)

Because there was no impurity in Jesus, He saw God clearly. Let this sequence be carefully noted and understood: What our minds engage greatly affects the way we feel, and how we feel greatly influences the way we act. Our Lord's unclouded intelligence brought about a perfect consciousness of God that captured His whole heart and soul and mind. The One who saw God clearly loved Him perfectly. In Him there was no undivided affection.

Our Lord was no tight-lipped, unemotional ascetic. He rebuked hypocrites with burning but righteous anger – righteous because it was not a grudge at what was happening to Him but grief at what was happening to others. He looked upon a young ruler and loved him. He could rejoice in spirit and on occasions was moved with compassion.

Visualise Him at the graveside of Lazarus when He came face-to-face with His friend's death. How did He react on that sad occasion? He responded surprisingly with two strong emotions. The first was angry indignation. In John 11:33–34, we read:

When Jesus saw her weeping, and the Jews who had come along with her also weeping, he was deeply moved in spirit and troubled. "Where have you laid him?" he asked.

The phrase "deeply moved in spirit" is translated from the Greek verb *enebrimesato*, which means, literally, "snorted". The New Testament scholar C.K. Barrett, in his commentary on John 11, writes: "It is beyond question that *embrimasthai* implies anger." A careful study of the Greek leads to the conclusion that when Jesus approached the grave of Lazarus He did so fuming at the fact death had taken away one of His dear friends.

But another deep emotion stirred in His heart, too, the emotion of deep sorrow and compassion. This is clear from the phrase "Jesus wept" (v.35). The tears He shed were not tears of anger but of sadness and sorrow for the predicament of the two sisters, Martha and Mary. He felt indignation and compassion – two emotions that in His case were consistent with perfect love.

Many other windows in the Gospels let in a flood of light on our Lord's emotional nature. Watch His whole being shake with the emotion of grief and sadness as He beholds Jerusalem, the city He loved, hastening to its doom (Luke 19:41). Those tears were not just the perfect expression of Christ; they were also the perfect expression of God. The Saviour felt as God felt.

G. Walter Hansen wrote in *Christianity Today*:

> The Gospel writers paint their portraits of Jesus using a kaleidoscope of brilliant emotional colours. Jesus felt compassion, he was angry, indignant and consumed with zeal; he was troubled, greatly distressed, very sorrowful, deeply moved and grieved; he sighed, he wept and sobbed; he groaned; he was in agony; he was surprised and amazed; he rejoiced very greatly and was full of joy; he greatly desired and greatly loved.

The Man of unclouded intelligence was also the Man of undivided affection. He reflected the image of God without any deficiency or distortion.

An ancient philosopher said, "Anyone can become angry. That is easy. But to be angry with the right person, to the right degree, at the right time, for the right purpose, and in the right way – that is not easy" (attributed to Aristotle). That is the challenge for us, but for Jesus it was no challenge.

Our Lord was perfect in His emotional make-up.

OUR LORD'S VOLITIONAL MAKE-UP

In this analysis of the perfect personality of Jesus, we must remind ourselves again of the interaction of mind, emotion and will. Seeing God clearly and loving Him perfectly, He gave Himself to Him unreservedly. Our Lord's will was one with the will of His Father.

It was, of course, ever so. Paul in Philippians 2:4–7 tells us:

Each of you should look not only to your own interests, but also to the interests of others. Your attitude should be the same as that of Christ Jesus: Who, being in very nature God, did not consider equality with God something to be grasped, but made himself nothing, taking the very nature of a servant, being made in human likeness.

More is revealed here than just His attitude of mind; we see also the act of will by which the change from heaven to earth was wrought. In the face of tremendous need, He did not hold onto or grasp His right of equality, but for the purposes of your salvation and mine He abandoned the privileges of the eternal throne to take upon Himself human flesh.

The action of His will is seen in those strange but sublime words "but made himself nothing". The Eternal Word came from the bosom of the Father to the body of a woman, from a position where He had infinite expression to a state where He was limited in so many ways. The Word passed from controlling the universe to obedience, from independent co-operation in the equality of Deity to dependent submission to the will of God.

Our Lord's spiritual nature was evidenced by His unceasing recognition of God. His mental capacity is manifest in the marvellous majesty of His dealing with all problems. His physical life was seen moving along the line of the purely human in weariness, hunger, method, sustenance and seasons of rest.

His will was seen as always choosing the principle of divine activity, always moving towards the goal of pleasing God. In Romans 15:3, Paul tells us Christ did not please Himself. Our Lord Himself said on one occasion, "I seek not to please myself but him who sent me" (John 5:30).

Jesus also said, "'My food is to do the will of him who sent me and to finish his work'" (John 4:34). Every movement and decision of the will of Jesus, under the constraint of the divine will, are a revelation of the action and method of the will of God, under the constraint of eternal love. In Jesus we have a picture of a will yielded to the divine will in a way that is absolutely stupendous. In everything He did he sought always to please the Father.

The will, it is believed by almost all theologians, is the citadel against which all the forces of temptation are directed. And because our Lord had unclouded intelligence and undivided affection, His will was unswerving when it came to obeying the commands of God. In John 8:29, He said,

> *The one who sent me is with me; he has not left me alone, for I always do what pleases him.*

Clearly Christ had a will of His own because He drew a distinction between His will and His Father's will. Our Lord was perfect in the way He willed.

OUR LORD'S RELATIONAL STYLE

Perhaps nowhere is our Lord's perfection seen more clearly than in the way He related to people. In the Gospels, we see Jesus often surrounded by crowds. Over and over again we read statements like this: "The people thronged around him." "They could not get near to him because of the crowd." "The multitude followed him." Early in His ministry, except on those occasions when He withdrew to pray, He seems always to be in the midst of a crowd.

It is said that children quickly sense the nature of an individual and are drawn to those who are warm and friendly. Watch how Jesus related to children. They flocked to Him, and He gathered them in His arms.

Watch, too, how He related to women. The Gospels are rich in incidents of Jesus in touch with women – and never does He imply their inferiority. He treated them with respect. Our Lord was born among a people who took a low view of women. A Jew would not greet a woman on the street much less talk with her there. In morning prayer a Jew thanked God that he was not made a Gentile, a slave or a woman. It was impious for a Jew to teach a woman.

Yet in all the contacts Jesus made with women, He was always respectful. Picture Him by the well at Sychar. Jesus, tired, sat by the well. His disciples had gone away to buy food. When they returned, they "marvelled" (John 4:27, NKJV). Why? Because He was talking to a woman who was a Samaritan. The woman was staggered herself when Jesus addressed her.

Picture Him again in the Temple when they bring before Him a woman caught in adultery. It was a trap and a clever one at that. If He had said, "Stone her," He could have been accused of encroaching on the rights of the Romans, who alone had the authority of life and death. If He had said, "Let her go," then He would have been contravening the Law of Moses, which made death the penalty for adultery. He said neither. Instead He said, "Let the one without sin cast the first stone." And one by one they slunk away. Only Jesus could have said that and achieved the effect. But don't let that incident make you think He was soft on sin. His last words to her were these: "Neither do I condemn you. Go now and leave your life of sin" (John 8:11).

On one occasion they called our Lord "a friend of tax collectors and 'sinners'" (Luke 7:34). Does that mean He overlooked people's sin in order to build friendships with them? Of course not. People sensed that the Saviour was not against them for their sin; He was for them against their sin.

Look also at how He related to His disciples. They were all ordinary men. We know the occupations of only five of the twelve. Four were fishermen and one was a tax collector. A tax collector in those days corresponded to a greedy moneylender today. Yet He took these men and, through His relationship with them, made them – with the single exception of Judas Iscariot – into men who became a powerful force in the establishing of His Church.

The thought could easily escape us, but Christianity, in fact, began in a relationship – the relationship between Christ and His disciples. Mark's Gospel says, "He appointed twelve – designating them apostles – that they might be with him and that he might send them out to preach" (Mark 3:14). Note the words "that they might be with him". The first part of their calling was not to preach but to be with Him – relationships.

The way in which our Lord built strong relationships with His disciples can be seen most clearly in an incident recorded for us in John 6. Christ had presented a challenging message to the crowd who had gathered to listen to Him. He talked about the fact that those who followed Him must be prepared to "eat his flesh and drink his blood".

The figure of speech He used was not understood by the people and obviously they were offended by it. "From this time many of his disciples turned back and no longer followed him" (v.66). The passage in John 6 continues: " 'You do not want to leave too, do you?' Jesus asked the Twelve. Simon Peter answered him, 'Lord, to whom shall we go? You have the words of eternal life. We believe and know that you are the Holy One of God' " (vv.67–69).

It was a critical moment in the Master's career. The crowds who had flocked to hear Him were melting away, upset by His hard sayings. Reading the unspoken thoughts of His immediate band of disciples, Jesus brought the issue out into the open by asking, "You do not want to leave too, do you?"

Seen against such a background, Peter's answer is magnificent. Peter realised that there was no one quite like Jesus. He had walked with Him and seen Him in all kinds of situations and circumstances, and never once had the Saviour revealed any character flaws or committed any sin. Here was someone who related to God and others not just effectively but perfectly. Is it any wonder that Peter responded the way he did? "Lord, to whom shall we go? You have the words of eternal life."

One writer defines *Christianity* as "the science of relating well to others in the spirit of Jesus Christ". Never did anyone reveal the true nature of relationships like Jesus.

OUR LORD'S PHYSICAL PERFECTION

Consider with me, finally, the physical perfection of Jesus. It cannot be proved from Scripture, but I hold that Jesus was perfect in physical form and proportion. Those who object quote Isaiah's words found in chapter 53 of his prophecy:

He had no beauty or majesty to attract us to him, nothing in his appearance that we should desire him. (v.2)

What Isaiah is telling us is not that Christ lacked physical beauty but rather that men and women would be blind to His inner beauty – the beauty of His character.

If the body is the outer and visible sign of the inner and visible spirit, then the perfect spirit of Jesus expressed itself through a perfect physical frame.

In Him, too, was an absence of disease. He had strength enough for the work of the day. Although at times we see Him tired and weary (for example at the well of Sychar in John 3:6), His tiredness was a natural one because of physical demands such as walking great distances, not the tiredness that comes through a vexed spirit.

Is this claim that Jesus was perfect in everything one that can be proved from Scripture? Indisputably so. Three times in the New Testament God opened the heavens above His Son to affirm Him. The first occasion was at His baptism in the River Jordan (Matt. 3:17). The second was at the moment of His Transfiguration (Matt. 17:5). The third was when He was drawing near to the cross and a small contingent of men from Greece came to speak to Him (John 12:28).

I am reminded of the story concerning Grieg, the great Norwegian composer. He was staying in a hotel in Oslo on one occasion when in the next room he heard a woman practising one of his compositions. He listened for a while, and being impressed with both the quality of her voice and her rendering of his work, he could contain himself no longer. Knocking on the door, he startled the woman who answered by shouting excitedly, "That is how my songs should be sung!" God did something of the same thing in relation to His Son when He was here on earth. Three times He shouted down from His cloudy pulpit as if to say, "That is how my life should be lived!"

Through the coming of Jesus Christ into this world and by way of His perfect personality, God revealed Himself anew to humankind in such a way to appeal to our emotion, which in turn leads to the submission of our will.

A wonderful verse in Romans 8:29 says this:

> *For those God foreknew he also predestined to be conformed to the likeness of his Son, that he might be the firstborn among many brothers.*

In the original Greek the word *conformed* is *summorphos*, which means "having the same form". And what form is that? It is the form of Jesus Christ. And what form does He bear? Paul answers that in Philippians 2:6–7.

Who, being in very nature [the form of] God, did not consider equality with God something to be grasped, but made himself nothing, taking the very nature of a servant, being made in human likeness.

It is to that image that God has predestinated us to be conformed. Just as the first Adam produced a son in his own likeness and after his image (Gen. 5:3), so the Last Adam, throughout this age of grace, is producing a progeny bearing a moral and spiritual resemblance to Himself. The Fall marred God's image in man, and Jesus' purpose is to restore it.

To quote G. Campbell Morgan once more:

The only conception of God that man has, is what he finds within himself, and in attempting to think of God, he has consciously or unconsciously always projected his own personality into immensity. This would have been a true thing for him to do had he remained true to the Divine ideal, for he was created in the image of God. Seeing that shadow had become blurred and the image defaced, in the projection of himself man has emphasized the defects and intensified the ruin. To correct that God became incarnate, stooped to the level of man's power to comprehend Him, gave him a perfect Man in order that the lines projected from the perfect personality into immensity might be true lines and so reveal the facts concerning Himself.

Jesus is God's perfect man. Every fact of His wisdom reveals the wisdom of God's working in harmony with Him. Every manifestation of the love of His heart is the revelation of a mind given over to God, a heart that is fully in love with Him and a will working under the constraint of eternal love.

Through Him Deity takes hold on humanity. Through Him humanity takes hold of Deity.

Chapter 10

RESTORING THE IMAGE

E. Stanley Jones tells the story of a little boy who one Christmas Day stood for several minutes before a picture of his absent father and then turned to his mother and said wistfully: "How I wish Father would step out of the picture." A similar cry must have arisen in the heart of all those who lived in Old Testament times, who believed in God and longed for His appearing.

One day the Father stepped out of the picture. He stepped out at Bethlehem. John's Gospel says simply but sublimely:

> *The Word became flesh and dwelt among us.*
> (John 1:14, NKJV)

He also said:

> *No-one has ever seen God, but God the One and Only, who is at the Father's side, has made him known.*
> (John 1:18)

Our Lord's coming into this world gave us a true picture of what God is like and reflected His image to us. What I am now about to say may seem strange, but the truth is in the perfect life of Jesus of Nazareth we see a lot of God, but we do not see all we need to see. It took something more than a perfect life to reveal God fully.

THE MAGNETISM OF THE CROSS

Consider this important verse, one of the most significant statements our Lord ever uttered:

> *So Jesus said, "When you have lifted up the Son of Man, then you will know that I am the one I claim to be."* (John 8:28)

Jesus was speaking to the Jews, saying in effect, "You may not see God in Me now as I live and work among you. Your eyes are blinded by bigotry and unbelief. But a time will come when you will see God in Me. As I hang upon a Roman cross, then shall I lay completely bare the heart of the Eternal and reveal the beauty and perfection of His being. You will see God in Me *then!*"

Solemnly I say, it took a cross to reveal God fully.

When we watch Jesus speaking such words of wisdom, healing the sick, causing the lame to walk, giving sight to the blind, showing us the compassion and love of God, we do not see all there is of God. Certainly we see something of Him. When the disciple Philip rather naively enquired of Christ: "Lord, show us the Father and that will be enough for us" (John 14:8); Jesus, apparently astonished by the request, replied:

> *"Don't you know me, Philip, even after I have been among you such a long time? Anyone who has seen me has seen the Father."* (v.9)

Looking at our Lord's earthly life, we behold in many wonderful ways the character and personality of God – holiness, purity, humility, love. But again I say, we do not see all there is to see. That unfolding comes only at the cross.

Here's an illustration that might help. Imagine a great concert pianist attempting to play the Warsaw Concerto on a toy piano. The musical genius would be present, but the expression would be limited by the instrument. But now think of the same musician sitting before a modern grand piano. At once all his powers come into play, and as he weaves the melodies, you say to yourself, "Ah, what a great musician. The grand piano reveals him."

In much the same way the cross reveals the heart of God. Listen to His words again, this time from the Amplified New Testament:

> *"When you have lifted up the Son of Man on the cross you will realise that I am He for Whom you look."* (John 8:28)

It is interesting, although too much must not be made of it, that Deity is never ascribed to Jesus Christ until after His crucifixion. Before that He was called the Messiah and the Son of God but never actually God Himself. That realisation came to Thomas as he stood on the other side of Calvary. Confronted by the realism of those revealing scars, he could not refrain from exclaiming, "My Lord *and my God!*" (John 20:28).

As Lillias Trotter so beautifully put it: "The world's salvation was not wrought out by the thirty years in which Christ went about doing good but in the three hours in which he hung, stripped and nailed in uttermost exhaustion of spirit, soul and body till his heart broke."

Had Jesus simply lived on this earth without giving His life on a cross, history would have recorded that One came among us who lived as God designed life to be lived. Great though that would have been, there would have been no power in it to restore us to the image of God.

The incarnation revealed God, but it took a cross to reconcile us to Him. The apostle Paul, when writing to the Colossians, put it like this:

Once you were alienated from God and were enemies in your minds because of your evil behaviour. But now he has reconciled you by Christ's physical body through death to present you holy in his sight, without blemish and free from accusation. (Col. 1:21–22)

The thought of reconciliation was in his mind when he wrote to the Romans:

For if, when we were God's enemies, we were reconciled to him through the death of his Son, how much more, having been reconciled, shall we be saved through his life! (Rom. 5:10)

Note carefully the order of words in the last text: "We were reconciled to him." Let no one think that He was reconciled to us. The truth is the other way round. Jesus did not die to make God love us; it was because God loved us that Jesus died.

Take another important statement that fell from the lips of Jesus:

"But I, when I am lifted up from the earth, will draw all men to myself." (John 12:32)

Some talk about the cross as a tragedy, but the surprising thing is that Jesus looked upon His elevation on the cross as the pinnacle of His achievement. He appeared to hold out His arms towards it more eagerly than any Olympic winner towards the tape. There is almost a glint of anticipation in His eye as He contemplates it, and right from the beginning of His ministry He seemed to sense that by His cross and through His cross there would be released an invisible magnetism that would lay siege to men's and women's hearts and draw them into the arms of a forgiving and reconciling God.

Jesus is God, and when He speaks of attracting men and women to Himself, He is really speaking of attracting them to His Father. This is the way reconciliation is effected. The cross is God's magnet to draw men and women to Himself and the power by which God's image can be restored in us.

NO SALVATION APART FROM THE CRUCIFIED CHRIST

Only a crucified Saviour could save us from our sins. The New Testament is clear on this point and comes back to it in different ways time and time again. We are saved and forgiven by and through our Lord's death on the cross. But couldn't God forgive sins without the necessity of Christ dying on a cross? The answer is no.

Almost every day our newspapers report crimes of every description – some too horrifying to read. Do we wave those things aside and say they are of no consequence? Of course not. Society attempts to seek out those responsible and bring them to account. How can we who witness such sins and refuse to wave them lightly aside suppose that God lightheartedly waves them aside? Any talk of God's lightly forgiving sin is sentimentalism.

The pillars of justice would fall in any society that views sin or crime lightly. Imagine a judge in a human court hearing a guilty man's professions of penitence with a kind word and a free pardon. "If you are sorry, then we will say no more about it. Be more careful in the future." No society could stand long where such judgments were common. God does not view our sin lightly; He sees it as a colossal debt. But because of His great undying love, He arranged for Christ to pay that debt on the cross.

It was because of the cross that we find in the New Testament a verse like this:

> *And we, who with unveiled faces all reflect the Lord's glory, are being transformed into his likeness with ever-increasing glory, which comes from the Lord, who is the Spirit.* (2 Cor. 3:18)

How does God go about the task of transforming us into the likeness of our Lord – restoring us to the divine image so that we begin to think like Him, feel like Him and choose like Him? There are three processes by which it is done. The first is called justification; the second, sanctification; and the third, glorification.

THE JOY OF JUSTIFICATION

Theologians point out that there is often an antiphonal relationship between the Old Testament and the New. The Old Testament, for example, raises the question, where is the Lamb? The New answers: "Behold the Lamb!" So it is also in relation to justification. Job raises the inquiry in Job 25:4 (KJV): "How then can man be justified with God?" The New Testament returns at least four replies. It says we are justified by grace (Rom. 3:24), justified by blood (Rom. 5:9), justified by Christ's resurrection (Rom. 4:25), justified by faith (Rom. 5:1).

What does it mean to be justified? "To beautify is to make beautiful; to pacify is to make peaceful; to justify is to make just." It means to make consciously right not on the basis of one's own efforts but on what Christ accomplished on the cross.

The clever evangelical cliché that to be *justified* means to be "just as if I had never sinned" is far too negative. The word implies something positive – that not only have we been exonerated, acquitted, absolved, but that it is as if we had actually lived the life that Jesus lived. It means we are credited with Christ's life and power. Justification means much, much more than mere forgiveness.

Justification is an act of grace. It is not our merit that brings us salvation but God's mercy and favour. John Stott asked: "If God justifies sinners freely by his grace, on what ground does he do it? How is it possible for the righteous God to declare the unrighteous to be righteous without either compromising his righteousness or condoning their unrighteousness? God's answer is the cross."

In the Koran, John Stott points out, the forgiveness of a merciful God is mentioned, but forgiveness is always given to the meritorious whose good works have been weighed in Allah's scales. The good news of the gospel is that through Christ, mercy is given to the undeserving, those whose merits could never be weighed in God's scales.

We have fallen short of the glory of God, the standard of righteousness. He cannot overlook sin, but He can look over it to Calvary where Jesus died. We need help to be justified, and this help is provided for us in the cross.

In *How to Be Born Again*, Billy Graham pictures a courtroom scene that effectively captures the great truth underlying justification.

> Picture a courtroom. God the judge is seated in the judge's seat, robed in splendor. You are arraigned before Him. He looks at you in terms of His own righteous nature as it is expressed in the moral law. He speaks to you:
>
> God: John (or) Mary, have you loved me with all your heart?
>
> John/Mary: No, your honor.
>
> God: Have you loved others as you have loved yourself?
>
> John/Mary: No, your honor.
>
> God: Do you believe that you are a sinner, and that Jesus Christ died for your sins?
>
> John/Mary: Yes, your honor.
>
> God: Then your penalty has been paid by Jesus Christ on the cross and you are pardoned. Because Christ is righteous and you believe in Christ I now declare you justified.

This is what it means to be justified.

Justified freely by his grace through the redemption that came by Christ Jesus. God presented him as a sacrifice of atonement, through faith in his blood. He did this to demonstrate his justice, because in his forbearance he had left the sins committed beforehand unpunished – he did it to demonstrate his justice at the present time, so as to be just and the one who justifies those who have faith in Jesus. (Rom. 3:24–26)

THE SWEETNESS OF SANCTIFICATION

A second movement in the process of restoring us to the divine image is called *sanctification*. It is the *process* by which Christ makes us into the image of God. It takes but a moment for justification to take place, but it takes a lifetime for our souls to be shaped in the image of Christ.

Sanctification is a consequence of justification, but it must not be regarded as automatic. Some Christians behave badly after being converted. They insist on having their own way, make no attempt to relate well to others, and ignore many of the principles for living that God lays down in His Word, the Bible. This is why so much Scripture is about behaving as God wants us to behave, passages about controlling the tongue, working for a living, being honest and forgiving, being hospitable, and duties between husbands and wives, masters and servants. As the Old Reformers used to put it: "The law sends us to Christ to be justified, and Christ sends us back to the Law to be sanctified."

I once heard a preacher ask children this question: "What is the greatest thing anyone can be on this earth?" Answers included an astronaut, a multimillionaire, an inventor, a military leader, a nurse and an engineer. "No," said the preacher, "the greatest thing anybody can ever be on this earth is to be like Jesus."

God has put His Holy Spirit within us, says Paul, to make us holy.

For God did not call us to be impure, but to live a holy life. Therefore, he who rejects this instruction does not reject man but God, who gives you his Holy Spirit. (1 Thess. 4:7–8)

The Spirit is at work in every committed Christian to help us subdue our fallen, selfish human nature and to cause Christ's character to be revealed in us. He is attempting to transform us by degrees into the image of Christ so that more and more we begin to think as Christ thinks, feel as He feels and choose as He would choose.

Several years ago there was a story in the British newspapers that told of Queen Elizabeth's commissioning two portraits of herself. One was by Annigoni, the celebrated Italian artist; the other was by the world famous photographer Karsh of Ottowa. Both were beautiful portraits, but there was a marked difference between them, and that was the way they were produced.

For Annigoni's portrait numerous sittings had to be arranged at the palace. Her majesty posed for the artist, who stood before her with his canvases, his palette and his brushes. Touch by touch of paint was transferred by the hand of the artistic genius from the palette to the canvas, and gradually the royal image emerged.

What a contrast was presented by Karsh. All he had to do was to arrange one sitting and, when he was ready, to press a button on his highly sophisticated camera, and in a moment he had several exact likenesses of the Queen on celluloid! The former process is analogous to what is technically called in Scripture sanctification, a method whereby redeemed mankind is gradually restored to the image by his Maker.

The great preacher, Samuel Rutherford, wrote: "The question uppermost in my mind is whether Christ is more to be loved for giving sanctification or for free justification?"

Just as the First Adam begat a son in his own likeness, so the Last Adam is throughout this age of grace producing a progeny that reflects the beauty of Jesus.

THE GRANDEUR OF GLORIFICATION

The final procedure is glorification. This will take place when we are transformed in a flash into the likeness of our Lord. This is how the apostle John puts it:

> Dear friends, now we are children of God, and what we will be has not yet been made known. But we know that when he appears, we shall be like him, for we shall see him as he is. (1 John 3:2)

In relation to glorification the second coming will put the finishing touches to the portrait of Christ in us. The life of grace will end in the likeness of glory.

> Grace all the work will crown
>   Through everlasting days.
> It lays in heaven the topmost stone
>   And well deserves the praise.

The world has known only one man who is perfect – Jesus. Billy Graham states that you can't find a perfect Christian anywhere in the world. Paul confessed to personal imperfection:

> Not that I have already obtained all this, or have already been made perfect, but I press on to take hold of that for which Christ Jesus took hold of me. (Phil. 3:12)

Suppose I give you a leather Bible. You take it and say, "Now it's mine." But it's not yours until you study it, pore over its pages and acquaint yourself with its great themes. So it is with sanctification. The moment we take Christ as our sanctification, we are perfect and complete in Him (Col. 4:12). But it will require your lifetime to work it out. There are many ministries, the Holy Spirit, the Word of God, disciplines of life, personal devotions and public worship.

A PERSONAL INVITATION

The great William Law, John Wesley's one-time teacher, said on one occasion, "A Christ not in us, is a Christ not ours." It occurs to me that someone reading this book may profess to be a Christian but has never personally received Jesus Christ into his or her life by an act of faith and commitment. If that is so, then lovingly I say it: A Christ not in you is a Christ not yours. If you have never received Jesus Christ into your life as your personal Lord and Saviour, then permit me to spell out for you the steps you need to make this a reality.

Incredible though it may sound or seem to those who have not yet realised it, God (the great God of the universe) will come by invitation and enter into a relationship with any man or woman. This invitation is open to people in all walks of life – business people or just busy people, the rich, the poor, the educated, the uneducated. All may come.

For nearly two thousand years Jesus Christ has been coming into the lives of men and women and transforming them. Some of the first to receive Him were fornicators and adulterers, perverts, thieves, swindlers, drunkards and foul-mouthed men. If this suggests that His transforming power is applicable only to those who might be described as the down-and-outs, let me make clear that He is for the up-and-outs too. Everyone needs the change Christ offers, for He is the supreme specialist in making men and women whole.

It is a mistake to think that only certain types of people can come to know God. Everyone has built-in longings for Him, and we have only to reach out to Him through His Son, Jesus Christ, and He will be there. No one is constitutionally unable to find God; if we cannot find Him, the cause is not in our constitution but in our unwillingness to consent to being found.

Think how extraordinary it is that anyone can enter into fellowship with the Creator. Some consider the Christian faith to be simply about making a commitment to behave in ethical ways, but it is much, much more. Essentially it is a relationship. We can understand how a music lover enters into a new realm by sound and an art lover enters into a new world by colour, but to enter a realm where God becomes close and real and intimate is something too awesome for the human mind to contemplate. Yet millions all over the world know it to be true. And now it can come true for you.

Let's be clear what we mean by "knowing God". It is much more than knowing about God in the sense that we might know about the existence of the North and South Poles. It is an intimate and close knowledge such as one might have with a close and dear friend. We can gain some knowledge of God by looking at His creation, but intimate knowledge comes only as we open ourselves to an encounter with Him through His Son, Jesus Christ.

FIVE STEPS TO KNOWING GOD THROUGH CHRIST

What are the steps we must take in order to come to an intimate knowledge of God? There are five of them. I shall make them plain because we are coming now to the greatest and most important decision a person can make in this life. Someone has described the decision to open oneself to God as "the master decision", a decision that shapes all other decisions down the line. In psychology there is what is called "a major choice", a choice that doesn't have to be made over and over again every day.

This assumes of course that you will want to follow these steps, for God comes in only by invitation. The Creator never bludgeons His way into any person's life. He has made us free and He respects the personality He has made. God is eager and indeed *longing* to have a relationship with you, but He will never intrude where

He is not welcome. Those who want Him must first decide that they really want Him, and want Him for keeps.

Here then are the steps for knowing God.

First, consider carefully the implications of what is involved in entering into a relationship with God. You might, for example, have to break with some things when you open your life to Him. Issues or practices that are plainly evil cannot continue when you come to God through Jesus Christ. Note that I say *plainly* evil; by that I mean those things of which the New Testament clearly disapproves like adultery, lying and cheating. This is not to say that a man or woman who chooses to follow Christ will not slip. But a slip is different from a harboured evil. When true Christians slip or sin, they don't wallow in their sin but confess that they have erred, receive Christ's forgiveness and then go on – humbler, wiser, more careful and more dependent on their Lord. There is a cost to becoming a follower of Jesus Christ, but the rewards are infinitely worth more than the cost.

Look upon your commitment to God through Jesus Christ not merely as a surrender of your personality to His but as an *unconditional* surrender. The full title given to Jesus Christ in the Bible is the *Lord Jesus Christ*. The word *Lord* means that He is in full and total control of the universe. That is precisely the kind of control He wants to have in your life also. Now you should not draw back because of this. Think of it from this perspective: If Christ is to come and live in you, think in you, and will in you, then He can only do so if He is given access to your personality in as full a way as possible.

This does not mean you are expected to be a nonentity or a cipher. It means that your life intermingles with His, your thoughts intermingle with His, your will intermingles with His. But whenever your thoughts or your will clash with His, then His thinking and His will must prevail. This is the kind of commitment Christ asks of you. Do you consider this too hard, too demanding? Then think of what you get in return. The forgiveness of your sins, God's life in yours, the certainty of His presence, help in every problem you face and the guarantee of being with Him one day in heaven. And as you will discover, there are a host of other things too.

Once you are sure that you want God to come into your life, the second step is this – complete honesty and humility. As you reflect on making the decision to enter into a personal relationship with God, you will be tempted to be defensive, for it is hard not to defend your previous life patterns. But be relentlessly honest. Look at the issues objectively and see not what you might be losing but what you are about to gain.

A certain humility is also required in order to know God. One of the reasons we find it difficult to be humble is because of the perceived threat to our pride. Few words are as confusing as *pride* in the English language, because on the one hand it can mean "self-respect" and on the other "arrogance or haughtiness". The pride that is condemned in the Bible is the arrogant stance we take that puts the ego at the centre of our lives instead of God. Nothing permanent can happen at the core of our beings until the ego capitulates to the claims of God.

The reason I say that the second step in coming to know God should be that of absolute honesty and humility is because I know from experience how this ugly self-centred being of ours will plead, excuse and rationalise. It will allow marginal changes but will do its utmost to stay at the centre. There can be no real encounter with God until we have the courage to face the sense of helplessness that comes when we realise we are being asked to give up the self and move through those feelings to have the self replaced by God.

The third step in knowing God is a willingness to repent of the commitment to independence that lies deeply embedded in all our hearts. This desire to run our lives independently of God must be acknowledged before we can turn to dependence on God. Without a humble recognition of our need to repent, a true encounter with God cannot take place. We have to face the reality of how our stubborn commitment to independence has hurt our Creator. Repentance involves being genuinely sorry about that.

You cannot make your way along the road that leads to God unless you are willing to acknowledge that you have spurned God and put yourself rather than Him at the centre of your life. Enter into the sadness of that fact. This is what repentance is, saying you are sorry to God for having chosen to run your life on your own terms instead of choosing His.

The fourth step in knowing God is the acceptance of God's full and free forgiveness. Everyone needs forgiveness, for as the Bible puts it:

There is no-one righteous, not even one ... There is no difference, for all have sinned and fall short of the glory of God. (Rom. 3:10, 22–23)

Human beings commit three types of offences. One is an offence against another person. Another is an offence against society. The third is an offence against God. The offence that needs forgiveness is the offence committed against God through maintaining an attitude of independence.

Only God can forgive this kind of sin. This is one of the prerogatives of Deity. That was how people first began to realise that Jesus Christ was God on earth: He forgave sins. So open your heart to receive the great gift of forgiveness. Allow no pride to hinder you. Don't pretend that you are better than you are. Look again at the cross. Christ died so that you might be forgiven. So go to Him now and by faith take from Him the forgiveness of your sins. And take it with wonder and delight.

The fifth and final step on the road to knowing God is to trust God to be all that He has promised to be. *Trust* is really another word for *faith*. Basically they mean the same thing. Listen to what the Bible has to say about faith:

And without faith it is impossible to please God, because anyone who comes to him must believe that he exists and that he rewards those who earnestly seek him. (Heb. 11:6)

Some people think faith is peculiar to religion, but actually simple faith is found in almost every area of life. Whenever you board a bus, you exercise faith – faith that the driver knows his job. When you go to a restaurant for a meal, you exercise faith – faith that the food has been hygienically prepared and properly cooked. When you send your child to school, you have faith – faith that the teacher will not poison your child's mind. Commerce and industry operate by faith; all business is built on credit. The word *credit* is simply the Latin form of *trust*.

If then faith is everywhere, it ought not surprise us to come across it on the road to knowing God. In order to know God, you must turn from self-centredness to putting your trust in Him. No one can properly learn to swim without getting into the water. Only experiment can end in experience. No one has ever learned to swim by theory alone.

When all the movements have been explained and demonstrated, the time comes when one has to get into the water and trust oneself to its supporting power. The mother who said that her little boy could not go in the water until he learned to swim was talking nonsense. Trusting the water is a necessary part of learning to swim. Decline to venture, and by your own act you cut yourself off from that kind of certainty.

So you are invited to venture. You need no human intermediary to know God. Any man or woman can go directly to God through Jesus Christ. Think of Christ, the Revealer and Reconciler to God, as close to you now. Talk to Him now in your mind. This is what we call prayer. It is the mind reaching out to God.

If it helps, you might like to pray the following prayer. If you decide to form your own prayer, then may I suggest you make sure it covers these elements: honesty, humility, repentance, acceptance of God's forgiveness and simple trust. In this way I believe you will come to know God. Remember, we can only draw near to God in Jesus.

A friend of mine, when describing how he became a Christian, put it this way: "I got down on my knees in utter humility, confessed the sin of keeping God out by my independence, repented of that and then accepted by faith God's forgiveness. It was as simple as that. Simple but so sublime."

So now if you are ready to pray this prayer, find a quiet spot where you will be uninterrupted, sit or kneel, and say these words sincerely from your heart.

O God my Father, I come to You now in the Name of Your Son, Jesus Christ. Thank You for revealing Yourself to the world through Him. Thank You, too, for what He did for all humankind on the cross.

You have made Yourself known to me, and as I sense Your presence on the threshold of my life, I open the doors of my inner being to let You come in. I surrender my life entirely into Your hands.

I make this choice, understanding the implications. I have learned how not to live; I want to learn now how to live. Forgive me for keeping You out of my life for so long. As I turn to You now in humility of heart, I know that as I reach up to You, You are reaching down to me.

Forgive my every sin. I receive that forgiveness now according to Your promise and realise that I am free of them through the sacrifice of Your Son on the cross. Help me to live a life that reflects Your love and power. Give me the courage to tell others that I have committed my life to You. I am now no longer my own. I belong to You. Thank You, heavenly Father. I offer this prayer in the Name of Jesus Christ, Your Son and my Saviour. Amen.

Here's a final promise from the Scriptures for you.

"You will seek me and find me when you seek me with all your heart." (Jer. 29:13)

Chapter 11

STAYING ON COURSE

Billy Graham has often pointed out that it is not as a president but as a king that Christ wants to rule our lives. A president serves for a period of time and then goes out of office. A king rules for life. It is one thing to have Christ in our lives; it is another thing to let Him reside permanently at the centre.

Throughout time many people have professed to welcome Christ as King but then have sought to retain their own authority in certain areas of their lives. Then He is not *King*. "A truly kingly rule," I heard one preacher say, "is without limit, and it is that kind of rule He [Christ] asks us willingly to accept."

Jesus Christ wants to rule in us over the whole of our lives – home life, business life, social life, public life and, of course, the inner life. He is not willing to be shut out from even one part of our personalities.

Only as Christ and His principles are allowed to hold sway in every part of our lives can He empower us to live the life He designed for us. Surely this makes sense. If Jesus Christ is to empower us to live life the way it should be lived, then He cannot consent to be excluded from any territory that Satan could use.

Steven Covey, in *The Seven Habits of Highly Effective People*, likens the course of our lives to that of an aeroplane as it flies from one destination to another. Before the plane takes off, the pilots have a clear flight plan. They know where they are going, but during the course of the flight, wind, rain, turbulence, air traffic, human error and other factors act upon the plane, causing slight deviations to the flight plan. But barring extreme weather systems or the need to divert, planes usually arrive safely at their destination. This is because during the flight the pilots receive constant feedback from control towers, other aeroplanes, even the stars, which enable them to keep returning to the flight plan.

How can we stay on course in our Christian lives, dealing with all of life's issues in a way that reveals the inevitable consequences of Christ living within? That is the focus of this and the next chapter.

This does not mean that we will never encounter problems, but it will help us cope with them and turn the stumbling blocks into stepping-stones.

Human beings, we remind ourselves, are made up of four areas of functioning: we can relate, think, choose, feel, all within a physical frame. But while we can *think* of the various parts of human functioning separately, they are never separate in experience. At different times, different parts of our being may be uppermost, but all are always present. The most logical of persons is not always thinking. The most ardent lover is not always feeling. All parts of our being intermingle and there is a constant interaction among them.

So what steps do we need to maintain spiritual health and ensure that our personalities function in the way they were designed?

THE STARTING POINT

We must begin by thinking about the physical. Why make the starting point the physical and not the spiritual? Because when anything goes wrong in this part of our beings, it can have a direct influence on our thoughts and our moods. It follows that we ought, as far as possible, to do as much as we can to take care of the physical.

Several verses of Scripture might help bring this into focus:

He who does not use his endeavors to heal himself is brother to him who commits suicide. (Prov. 18:9, Amplified)

It is God's will that ... each of you should learn to control his own body in a way that is holy and honourable. (1 Thess. 4:3–4)

I do not run like a man running aimlessly; I do not fight like a man beating the air. No, I beat my body and make it my slave so that after I have preached to others, I myself will not be disqualified for the prize. (1 Cor. 9:26–27)

We made the point earlier that through the medium of the body, the health of the spirit is shown. The body is presented by the spirit, and through this devotion of the body, the spirit expresses itself in worship. Perhaps much of what we think is worship is negated when we violate the temple in which God dwells – when we abuse the body by overwork, stress and other things.

Some sicknesses we are powerless to do anything about, but as I heard one doctor say, "A Christian has no right to be sicker than he or she ought to be." We must commit ourselves, as far as we possibly can, to be good tenants of the Lord's property.

This is what C.S. Lewis said regarding the body in his *Letters to Malcolm: Chiefly on Prayer:*

> Mine has led me into many scrapes, but I've led it into far more. If the imagination were obedient the appetites would give us very little trouble. And from how much has it saved me! But for our body one whole realm of God's glory – all that we receive through the senses – would go unpraised. For the beasts can't appreciate it and the angels are, I suppose, pure intelligence. They understand colours and tastes better than our greatest scientists, but have they retinas or palates? I fancy the "beauties of nature" are a secret God has shared with us alone.

In the early years of my pastoral life, a church member had some strange views about his physical being. He told me that he despised his body, and when I questioned him over this, he said, "Yes, I hate my body, and it is quite biblical to do so. The physical part of us is vile and should be rejected. The apostle Paul despised his body, and so should we."

When I asked for a scriptural basis for his argument, he read me Paul's words in Philippians 3:21 in the Authorised Version. The AV uses the phrase: "our vile body". I pointed out to him that the word translated *vile* in the Authorised Version means "lowly" and that Paul was saying our present bodies – subject as they are to weakness – are indeed "lowly" compared to the higher and incorruptible bodies we shall be given in the resurrection.

To treat one's body with disrespect is to disrespect God. If the truth is faced, we treat our cars with more respect than our bodies. In his book *The Way to Power and Praise*, E. Stanley Jones, under the title "What Would the Body Say?" wrote:

> I have sometimes imagined a convention of bodies met to discuss their inhabitants. One body stands up and says: "I wish the man that occupies me knew how to live. He doesn't so I'm tied in knots half the time." Another body stands up and says: "The woman who inhabits me is afraid to live. She's always inventing ways to escape living. She drinks and smokes, hoping that will let her out. But each time I protest by a reaction into dullness and lethargy, she whips me up again. But it's all a losing game, and some day I'm going to quit protesting and I'm going to give up and die." It's too bad that these humans don't know how to live.

Another body stands up and says: "Look at my condition. I'm all black and blue inside – and I'm showing it on the outside too. The person who lives in me has taken to being resentful toward life and has a chronic grouch. You should see how my gastric juices refuse to flow under these conditions. And now this silly person is dosing himself with medicines and running from doctor to doctor, who can't find a thing wrong with me. I know what is wrong: I don't work very well with resentments. I like good will."

Literalists might object to this and say our bodies do not talk, but they do. They talk in the only language they know, the language of protest; and the protest shows itself through upset, disease and pain.

Here are some suggestions I have used when counselling to help people keep their bodies in good repair.

Get a regular physical checkup and, if possible, by someone who understands the holistic approach. We are not just bodies but souls, and what happens in the soul is important. Those who function only at the physical level are lost. If you do not believe me, for I have had no medical training, then listen to what the physican John Sarno says in his book *Healing Back Pain*:

I believe that all medical studies are flawed if they do not consider the emotional factor. For example, a research project dealing with the hardening of the arteries usually includes consideration of the diet (cholesterol), weight, exercise, genetic factors – but if it does not include emotional factors, the results in my view are not valid.

If physical weaknesses are discovered, consider how much may be caused by emotional functioning. Some problems are purely physical, though some believe that every physical problem is influenced in some way by the emotions. But be careful not to go to the other extreme – that all disease is mental and spiritual. That is grievous error.

Begin an exercise programme. Our bodies were made to move, and we must keep them moving as much as possible. Control your weight. Watch what is happening. And don't be like the person who said, "Whenever I feel the need for exercise, I lie down until it goes away." People who don't or won't exercise have little willpower.

Consider also the importance of nutrition. Eating the right foods is a necessary part of keeping fit. In his book *Abundant Living*, E. Stanley Jones quotes James S. McLester:

> In the past, science has conferred on those people who have availed themselves of the newer knowledge of infectious diseases, better health and a greater average of life. In the future, it promises to those races who will take advantage of the new knowledge of nutrition a larger stature, greater vigour, increased longevity and a higher level of cultural development.

Take vitamins. Jones also quotes Dr L. R. Greene:

> Life's chemical reactions are disturbed more frequently by a deficiency of vitamins than by any other cause. For instance a deficiency of Vitamin A gives rise to kidney, skin and gastrointestinal disorders, diarrhoea, poor appetite, bad teeth, chronic colitis, bronchitis, malnutrition followed by a greatly lowered state of general health and a high death rate from infectious diseases.

Watch what you eat. More than a millennium ago Hippocrates wrote: "Let your food be your medicine." Diet and nutrition are important. And watch your weight.

And, of course, consider that God heals. Some powerful words in the epistle of James are astonishingly ignored by some churches:

> *Is any one of you sick? He should call the elders of the church to pray over him and anoint him with oil in the name of the Lord. And the prayer offered in faith will make the sick person well; the Lord will raise him up. If he has sinned, he will be forgiven. Therefore confess your sins to each other and pray for each other so that you may be healed. (James 5:14–16)*

If your church doesn't practise that biblical injunction, then go to one that does. God heals today. I can tell you that I wouldn't be here today unless that were true.

UNDERSTAND YOUR LONGINGS

The truth that God made us as longing beings is one that has been strongly emphasised throughout this book. Deep in the heart of every one of us, we have been saying there are longings for relationship – first with the living God and then with other thinking, feeling, choosing beings like ourselves.

Because we are made in the image of God, everyone – even the most hardened atheist – reaches out to Him. They would not admit to this, of course, but as G.K. Chesterton said: "When a man knocks at the door of a brothel, he is really looking for God."

An atheist once said to me: "I don't believe in God, but I would like to, if only to satisfy the desire that seems to be within me for transcendence."

Understanding that we are longing beings and how to deal with those longings is crucial to keeping our lives on course spiritually. Permit me to lay down a few propositions to help you do that.

First, fix in your mind that you have longings within you that nothing on earth can satisfy. Multitudes have said if they only had this or that, they would always be happy. Some have died believing it. The evidence shows, however, that when they obtained what they believed would bring them happiness, they found that it satisfied for only a little while, and then there was the old persistent thirst back again, clamorous and as demanding as ever.

Alister McGrath in *Bridge Building* tells the story of Boris Becker, the noted tennis player who came close to taking his own life while overwhelmed with a sense of hopelessness and emptiness. Even though he was a tremendously successful tennis champion, he felt something was wrong:

> I had won Wimbledon twice before, once as the youngest player. I was rich. I had all the material possessions I needed: money, cars, women, everything ... I know that this is a cliché. It's the old song of the movie and pop stars who commit suicide. They have everything and yet they are unhappy ... I had no inner peace. I was a puppet on a string.

Some believe money will satisfy the ache that lies at the core of the human spirit. And some set their mind on a coveted position and believe obtaining it will bring them complete satisfaction. Fame – what Milton called "the last infirmity of noble minds" – is what appeals to others.

Still others seek pleasure, believing that will satisfy the ache in their soul. Lord Byron, whom one biographer described as "typical of the grosser hedonist", drifted in his search for pleasure from one woman to another and died an old man at the age of thirty-six. He said of himself on his last birthday:

> My days are in the yellow leaf;
>   The flowers and fruits of love are gone;
> The worm, the canker, and the grief
>   Are mine alone!

There are those also who believe that perfect physical health is what brings satisfaction. In our own day and generation, fitness has become almost a cult; but those who worship at its shrine fail to realise there are spiritual ills no harmony of the body can cure and, if they remain uncured, will rob the body of its health as well. That is the first fact: there is something in all of us that the best things on earth – husbands, wives, friends or health – cannot satisfy.

ACKNOWLEDGE YOUR LONGINGS

Here is a second truth: Only as you acknowledge your longings will you be able to move beyond them. Not to acknowledge unfulfilled longings is to be driven to search for satisfaction in other ways. One of the saddest things to behold is a Christian who remains content with practising the duties of the Christian life and relying on them to bring satisfaction rather than engaging in a dynamic and passionate relationship with God.

John Eldridge's statement bears quoting again at this juncture: "If Christianity does not take our breath away, then something else will." We will re-double our efforts in other directions (sometimes spiritual ones) to compensate for the lack of aliveness we feel in our souls.

A.W. Tozer said, "Thirsty hearts are those whose longings have been awakened by the touch of God within them." Listen to your heart. In *The Sacred Romance*, authors Brent Curtis and John Eldridge make this point most forcefully:

> Aren't you thirsty? Listen to your heart ... We join a small group and read a book on establishing a more effective prayer life. We train to be part of a church evangelism team. We tell ourselves that the malaise of spirit we feel even as we step up our religious activity is a sign of spiritual immaturity and we scold our heart for its lack of fervour ... The voice in our heart dares to speak to us again. Listen to me, there is something missing in all this. You long to be in a love affair, an adventure. You were made for something more. You know it.

The love affair and the adventure that these writers talk about can never be found in service for Christ, but in Christ and Christ alone. Do not misunderstand me: Our service for Him is important, but the most important issue in the Christian life is not what we do for Him but what He does for us. The deepest longings of our heart cannot be met except in a personal relationship with Jesus Christ.

Take this incident recorded in John's Gospel:

> On the last and greatest day of the Feast, Jesus stood and said in a loud voice, "If anyone is thirsty, let him come to me and drink. Whoever believes in me, as the

Scripture has said, streams of living water will flow from within him." (John 7:37–38)

The feast referred to here was the Feast of Tabernacles (2 Chron. 8:13; Ezra 3:4; Zech. 14:16), also called the Feast of Ingathering (Exod. 23:16; 34:22), and celebrated the dwelling in booths (or tabernacles), which were to be joyful reminders to Israel (Lev. 23:41; Deut. 16:14) of God's provision for them in the wilderness. It lasted for seven days (Lev. 23:36; Deut. 16:13; Ezek. 45:25), and on the eighth day they had a "closing assembly" when every Israelite lived in booths in commemoration of the fact that their fathers lived this way after their exodus from Egypt. Josephus referred to this feast as the holiest and greatest of the Hebrew feasts.

On the last day of the feast, the priest would go down to the pool of Siloam, draw water from it, then return to the Temple precincts and pour it into the dry earth, once again commemorating God's provision of water for His ancient people when they travelled through the wilderness.

Now against that background consider once again the words of John: "If anyone is thirsty, let him come to me and drink" (John 7:37). Note that when He uttered those words, they were said not in measured tones but in a "loud voice". It was not often that Jesus shouted. I imagine that more often than not He spoke in calm, measured tones. But on this occasion something moved His soul so deeply that He stood (in those days teachers usually sat) and shouted.

What was it that stirred our Lord so much that made Him stand up and cry out? Perhaps this: As the Saviour witnessed the pageantry and ceremony going on around Him and sensing that both people and priests were depending on the religious ritual rather than a personal relationship with the living God to satisfy their spiritual thirst, He was moved to shout out in their midst, "Come to Me and drink."

His voice still rings out across the centuries with the same message: Come to Me, he says, not to your wife, husband, friend or any other thing. I am the only One who can slake your thirst. Come to Me and drink.

That is the second fact: If we do not acknowledge our deep longings for God, we will remain satisfied with duty rather than devotion, with the things of Christ rather than with Christ Himself.

PEOPLE OF PASSION

The third truth is this: The only satisfying relationship with God is a passionate one. Several years ago, on the verge of retiring from active counselling, I sat down and began to think if a common denominator had been evident in the lives of the Christians who had sat in my counselling room asking for spiritual help. It did not take me long to conclude that one thing stood out above all others – lack of spiritual passion.

Many of these people were good Christians in many ways. They attended church, read their Bibles regularly, prayed, took care of their families and saw themselves as dutiful Christians, but they appeared to have so little passion in their lives.

Some were ministers who saw themselves more as performers than desperately thirsty servants needing to drink daily from *"the spring of living water"* (Jer. 2:13). I tell you again – with all the force and conviction of which I am capable – if we do not have a close and intimate relationship with God through His Son, Jesus Christ, no matter how dutiful we may be in observing the rules of Christian living, we will have little spiritual passion in our lives.

Whenever I peruse the words of the apostles John, Peter and Paul in the New Testament, I sense the passion for God that flowed through their hearts. Take the apostle John's words in the Revelation:

To him who loves us and has freed us from our sins by his blood, and has made us to be a kingdom and priests to serve his God and Father – to him be glory and power for ever and ever! Amen. (Rev. 1:5–6)

The words in our English translations do not bring out the flavour of the Greek. In the original language the words come across as a burst of impassioned thankfulness.

I can never read these words of John without thinking of a little poem quoted by Ian Macpherson in *This Man Loveth Me*. Poet W.S. Landor talks about a man who is near to dying and reflects on how his wife of just a few years will deal with his death. He pictures her coming to his graveside, paying her respects and then quickly moving on to other things:

> Proud word you never spoke, but you will speak
> For not exempt from pride some future day
> Resting on one white hand a warm wet cheek
> Over my open volume you will say
> This man loved me, then rise and trip away.

John seems to be saying the same thing: "This man loved me," he cries in effect. But he cannot rise and trip away. He must go on to worship.

The apostle Peter also speaks with passion in several sections of his epistles. Take this verse for example:

> *Praise be to the God and Father of our Lord Jesus Christ! In his great mercy he has given us new birth into a living hope through the resurrection of Jesus Christ from the dead, and into an inheritance that can never perish, spoil or fade – kept in heaven for you, who through faith are shielded by God's power until the coming of the salvation that is ready to be revealed in the last time.*
> (1 Pet. 1:3–5)

As he talks about God's great overflowing mercy vouchsafed to us in Christ, can you not sense the joy bubbling up within his soul? Peter was not just a dutiful follower of the Master. He was one of His impassioned disciples. Praise and gratitude overflow from him simply because they must.

Paul was a man of passion also. Whenever I read his letter to the Romans, I am intrigued when I read that after dealing with the most taxing theology, his heart overflows in gratitude to God. Theology turns to doxology as he contemplates all that God has done for us in Christ. Listen to him as he pauses for a moment to allow the feelings in his soul to find expression:

> *Oh, the depth of the riches of the wisdom and knowledge of God! How unsearchable his judgments, and his paths beyond tracing out! "Who has known the mind of the Lord? Or who has been his counsellor?" "Who has ever given to God, that God should repay him?"* (Rom. 11:33–35)

These New Testament writers were head over heels in love with Jesus Christ. Their pens seem to catch fire as they tell how His passion fired their passion. That is the third fact: Nothing will satisfy our soul like a passionate relationship with Jesus Christ.

TUNE IN TO YOUR LONGINGS

My next point is this: Tune in to your longings. This means more than just acknowledging them. It means getting in touch with the fact that you are a thirsty, longing being. Focus on that fact and feel that thirst. Our desire to know God and enjoy Him depends on how aware we are of what we lack. The more deeply we feel our thirst, the more deeply we will drink of Christ and the more eagerly we will be drawn to the source of true satisfaction. So tune in to the deep thirsts and the deep longings within your soul. If you are not willing to feel the deep longings that God has placed within you for Himself, you will live on the surface of life and come to believe that anything can satisfy it.

The words of Simone Weil, in her book *Waiting for God*, are pertinent and powerful:

> The danger is not lest the soul should doubt whether there is any bread, but lest by a lie, it should persuade itself that it is not hungry. It can only persuade itself of this by lying, for the reality of its hunger is not a belief but a certainty.

Whenever I have made this point to people in the past – to tune in to your deep longings – the first question they ask is, but how?

I suggest this: Take a sheet of paper and think of the times you have been disappointed in your life. Focus on how many times you have longed for someone to come through for you but they let you down. What were you longing for that was not met? How hurt were you in those moments? Was it because you depended too much on others to give you what your soul longed for?

Imagine, too, how you would handle such things as criticism, rejection or disappointment, if you were fully aware of how much you were loved by God. Was not the reason you were hurt so much because you looked to others and depended on them to meet the needs of your soul that only God can meet?

Does this mean that when we learn to rely on God for security, significance and self-worth that we no longer experience disappointment or need the love of others? No. We will still hurt, still be disappointed and still desire the affection and affirmation of others; but if and when it is not there – providing our relationship with God is intact – we can still go on; we can still function.

People may hurt us and let us down, but they cannot destroy us. Our engagement with a living God does not insulate us from feelings of hurt or make us invulnerable to disappointment, but it does uphold us so that we can go on loving others as our own souls are loved.

A word of caution: Tuning in to your deep longings must not become an obsessive exercise. I would describe it as something to be glanced at rather than to be gazed at. And be aware that tuning in to your longings will cause some uncomfortable feelings to rise within you. One such feeling will be that of helplessness. We saw earlier that the soul, because of the damage sin has caused, abhors the feeling of helplessness. Our carnal nature likes to feel it is in control, that it can meet the soul's demands through self-effort. It can't, but it likes to feel it can. Nothing is more humbling than a recognition of a thirst that only God can quench.

Another uncomfortable feeling that will arise is a sense of dependency. It is uncomfortable because God has made us dependent beings, but sin reverses that and works to make us feel independent. The soul, because of its fallen condition, hates to feel dependent; and yielding control for our soul's function to God is not easy. But it must be done.

It is not easy to face the fact that we are longing beings. To get in touch with the thirst in our souls means that things like helplessness and the sense of dependency surface and bring with them a challenge. This is why many people deny their longings and pretend they are not there. But denial exposes us all the more powerfully to their unnoticed tyranny.

My point is this: Trust God to meet your deepest longings. Turn from dependency on other things to dependence on Him. *Trust*, as we saw, is another word for *faith*. Sin is antitrust. I have met many people in the Christian life who can trust God with things like finance, healing and choice of a career but are unable to trust Him with their longings.

Here's a challenge we must face. Can we trust God to meet the deepest longings of our hearts, the longings for security, self-worth and significance, or do we turn to other things? To live a life of dependency on God means that we come before Him in absolute dependency, believing that if He doesn't come through for us, then we are sunk.

CHASING GOD

My final point is this: Learn to pant after God as did the psalmist. Take this brief selection of statements from the Psalms:

> As the deer pants for streams of water, so my soul pants for you, O God. My soul thirsts for God, for the living God. When can I go and meet with God? (Psa. 42:1–2)

> I spread out my hands to you; my soul thirsts for you like a parched land. (Psa. 143:6)

O God, you are my God, earnestly I seek you; my soul thirsts for you, my body longs for you, in a dry and weary land where there is no water. (Psa. 63:1)

Some time ago I read the comments of Paul Weaver, who briefly reviewed a book called *The God Chasers* by Tommy Tenney. He said: "I found the title particularly intriguing. After all, how can you chase God? I started reading the book and could not put it down. It challenged my life and whetted my appetite for more of God. *There is so much about God that I know so little about.*"

What does it mean to chase after God? Or as the psalmist put it, to pant after Him? It means several things. It means realising there is so much about God that I know so little about. The apostle Paul, a man who knew more about God than most, cries out in his epistle to the Philippians:

I want to know Christ and the power of his resurrection and the fellowship of sharing in his sufferings, becoming like him in his death. (Phil. 3:10)

Someone has said, "The beginning of education is the realisation of your ignorance." It is the same in the spiritual life. The beginning of spiritual development is the realisation of how little of God we know. Consider that, and let it whet your appetite to know more of Him.

Another thing that "panting after God" means is to make Him the soul's central focus. This means much more than attending church on Sunday, making sure you say your prayers before you go to sleep or occasionally reading a brief portion from the Scriptures. The pursuit of the soul after God calls for discipline and determination.

It means lingering before Him in prayer, feeding your soul as much as you can on His Word, meditating in that Word, and as a friend of mine puts it, "letting your soul loose to find its home in God". The New King James Version translates Psalm 63:8 this way: "My soul follows close behind You." He could well have said, "My soul chases after God."

A third thing that panting after God means is knowing Him for who He is, not just what He gives. Tommy Tenney says in his book that God Chasers are people who are more interested in the face of God than His hands. Christians, he claims, are so consumer-oriented that they are more interested in getting something from God than in knowing Him for who He is. God's purpose is for us to know Him intimately, to gaze upon His face, knowing that as we do, our soul will find Him to be its delight.

Ask yourself: "How deeply do I long after God? To what lengths am I prepared to go in order to know Him better?" The soul is capable of great passion; we see this in great music and great art. The truth is that none of us have been able to find in our relationships more than just a taste of what we long for. We were designed to be drawn, to pant after God. "But why is it necessary to acknowledge our deep longings and our deep thirst?" Because only thirsty people drink.

Keep ever before you, therefore, the thought that you are a longing being, with longings that only God can satisfy. If this constant awareness is not in your soul, then you will seek your satisfaction elsewhere. Let there be no doubt whatsoever about that.

Chapter 12

THREE VITAL ISSUES

Before we move on to consider how to stay on course in relation to the other three parts of our personality – the mind, the will and the emotions – we must pause to consider three important issues. Failure to understand and apply these issues can cause us to veer off course in our spiritual lives and subvert all our efforts to let Christ live His life in us.

But first, let me tell you about one of the great mistakes I made in the early days of my counselling. When someone shared a problem with me, my first approach was to try to discover how the problem might have arisen. I would first explore the physical area to see if a physical malfunction might be a contributing factor and a medical checkup necessary. Then I would explore the person's relationship with God, because I believed that if a problem has no physical basis it would have its basic cause in *misplaced dependency*, a failure to draw on Christ's power and energy for daily living.

I would then draw attention to the misplaced dependency, encourage the person to accept it and rely more on Christ's power, then go on to help him or her change their thinking, establish new goals and manage their emotions. By doing so, however, I unwittingly pushed people towards self-sufficiency and self-dependency and unwittingly contributed to the very problem I was trying to solve. This was because I failed to appreciate and integrate three vital issues into my counselling – issues that I have come to see are essential to effective Christian counselling as air is to the lungs.

Once I grasped the three issues I am now about to discuss and integrated them into my counselling, the change I saw in my counsellees was remarkable. The three issues I am referring to are these:

1. A clear understanding and awareness of sin
2. A willingness to own up to its reality in one's life
3. A turning away from it through real repentance.

These three things form what I call "The Dependency Dynamic". Unless we understand and are willing to apply these issues in our lives, then Christ empowered living will be more a theory than a fact.

WHATEVER HAPPENED TO SIN?

Focus with me first on the importance of a clear understanding and awareness of sin. *Sin* is a word that has almost vanished from the popular vocabulary. Cornelius Platinga, in his book *The Breviary of Sin*, says:

> The awareness of sin used to be our shadow. Christians hated it, feared it, fled from it, grieved over it. But the shadow has dimmed. ...
>
> Nowadays, the accusation "you have sinned" is often said with a grin, and with a tone that signals an inside joke. At one time the accusation still had the power to jolt people. Catholics lined up to confess their sins; Protestant preachers rose up to confess our sins. And they did it regularly. [As] a child growing up in the fifties I think I heard as many sermons about sin as I did about grace. The assumption in those days seemed to be that you couldn't understand either without understanding both.

Earlier we talked about sin in general terms. Now we must give it a sharper focus. It is no coincidence that the two main words in the Bible for *sin* are the Hebrew *chata* and the Greek *harmartia*. Both mean "missing the mark".

In *The Faith Once Delivered*, Ian Macpherson tells of a popular game in ancient times called Saints and

Sinners. The players lined up on sides, and the sport consisted of shooting arrows through a hoop hung at some distance from the archers. Those who got all their arrows through the hoop took their place among the saints; those who failed took their place among the sinners. In the game of life, however, there is no such thing as "natural" saints. Scripture says we have all come short of the glory of God (Rom. 3:23).

Gerald Kennedy, in a book called *Parables*, tells of an old man in Arkansas who was a compulsive sharpshooter. He would take pot shots at anything in sight. A skilled marksman following his trail was surprised always to find a bull's-eye. Wherever he went, he found signs of the sharpshooter's exploits – a barn door, a ranch fencing, or wherever – there was always a circle traced in white chalk and right in the centre a bullet hole.

This impressed the observer immensely. Meeting up with the old man, he complimented him on his superb marksmanship. The sharpshooter made light of it, and with a wave of his hand he dismissed it. "Shucks," he said, "'tain't nothing. I jess shoots first and draws a circle afterwards!"

Some people – Christians included – set up their own standards, and then they measure themselves by themselves, which, as the apostle Paul points out in his epistle to the Corinthians, shows lack of wisdom.

We do not dare to classify or compare ourselves with some who commend themselves. When they measure themselves by themselves and compare themselves with themselves, they are not wise. (2 Cor. 10:12)

Everyone, spiritually speaking, has missed the mark. A story comes down from the days of the Roman emperor Galerian that he once watched a man shooting arrows and said, "May I compliment you on your splendid talent for missing." That is a talent, if it may be called such, shared by the whole of humankind.

The Bible, as Cornelius Platinga points out, presents sin in an array of different images: missing a target, wandering from the path, straying from the fold, blindness, deafness, overstepping a line or failing to reach a goal – both transgressions and shortcomings.

However, I do not believe we can fully comprehend the nature of sin until we see it as self-centredness, the ego occupying the place God has reserved for Himself.

THE PERPENDICULAR PRONOUN

To spell *sin* properly we must always put the *I* in it. In fact, if we chop off the first and last letters of the word, what remains? *I*. See the letter in your imagination standing tall and stiff and starched. Raise it to almost cosmic proportions, and you have an idea how the human ego has disrupted created harmony.

Three texts in the New Testament, all written by the apostle Paul, bring this thought into focus.

I have been crucified with Christ and I no longer live,
but Christ lives in me. The life I live in the body, I live by
faith in the Son of God, who loved me and gave himself
for me. (Gal. 2:20)

But by the grace of God I am what I am, and his grace
to me was not without effect. No, I worked harder than
all of them – yet not I, but the grace of God that was
with me. (1 Cor. 15:10)

To the married I give this command (not I, but the
Lord): A wife must not separate from her husband.
(1 Cor. 7:10)

In each of these three texts the apostle Paul deliber-
ately draws his pen through the first-person singular.
"Yet not I," he says, crossing out the pronoun altogether.
Now that is not an easy thing to do.

A cartoon appeared in the British press many years
ago in which a worried-looking man was pictured sitting
at a typewriter with reams of paper piled high around
him, apparently unable to proceed. "It's no good," read
the caption, "I can't write my autobiography on this
machine, the capital I is missing."

If our lives are to be lived in the power of the
indwelling Christ, we are faced with an inescapable
challenge: Where will I place my dependency, on
Christ or self? Will I try to live life depending on my
own natural enthusiasm, or will I live it drawing
daily upon His strength, drinking daily of "the spring of
living water"?

THE ESSENTIAL NATURE OF SIN

John Wallace, principal of the Bible college where I was trained, used to say that we misapply the word *sin* when we attach it to such things as adultery, fornication, lying, stealing and cheating. These he claimed were really *sins*, the branches rather than the root. Sin is essentially self-dependency and self-sufficiency, trusting in one's own resources rather than in the resources of God. "You can chop off the branches," he used to say, "and yet still retain the trunk."

I like the way Dick Keyes put it in *Beyond Identity*:

> Sin is not always expressed in conscious animosity toward God. More often it is a polite relegation of God to irrelevance. Nevertheless it is still an expression of man's cosmic rebellion against his Maker – man taking his stance in independence from anything greater than himself.

We do not deal with sin effectively in our lives until we see it in the terms described by Dick Keyes. If you came and lived with me (I live alone since my wife died many years ago), you would find little wrong with the way I live the Christian life. But if you could look deep into my heart, you would see there, embedded like splintered glass, a stubborn commitment to independence – a tendency to rely on my experience, my expertise, to make my life work without having to trust God.

Some years ago a British magazine interviewed me in relation to the success of the daily devotional I write entitled *Every Day with Jesus* and headed their feature article thus: "Pastor with the World's Largest Daily Congregation". They put both the title and my photograph on their front cover. This title was used in the magazine because the Bible notes that I write are read by half a million people daily.

About the same time an old friend whom I had not seen for many years – a preacher – was due to visit me. I positioned the magazine on my coffee table so that as soon as he sat down he would catch sight of it. Suddenly the Holy Spirit spoke to my heart, and I wept as I realised what was happening.

For a few weeks previous to this incident I had been caught up in a round of Christian activity that had caused me to lose out on a close and intimate relationship with God. I had let down on my personal time with Him in prayer and allowed myself to be busier than God wanted me to be. Activity, even Christian activity, cannot fully satisfy. And because my relationship with God was not as close as it should have been, my soul was feeling somewhat parched. Here was an opportunity for a drink. I assumed my friend would see my photograph, ask to read the article and doubtless give me some affirmation.

What was I searching for at that time? I was looking for something to assuage the ache in my soul. I had moved from a daily dependence on God for my security, significance and worth and had transferred it to activity. But activity, even godly activity, can never satisfy the soul. Working for God is good, but that in itself cannot fully satisfy the soul.

There is joy in working for the Lord, of course, and some degree of satisfaction. But it does not fully satisfy. My goal at that moment was to get a little glory for myself, to impress. Realising this, I dropped to my knees, confessed and repented of the sin of misplaced dependency, and soon my soul thrilled once again with the completeness of the joy that comes from Jesus Christ.

Think a little more deeply about this terrible tendency in all of us to depend on our own resources rather than on God, to drink at leaky wells instead of coming to the spring of living water. What underlies this spirit of independence that seems to be so strongly rooted in us? I will tell you in a word – *pride.*

Pride persuades us that we belong to ourselves, and in order to maintain the dignity of our personality, we must not submit to anybody else. Pride stiffens the spirit. Pride is the deadliest disease of the soul. It builds barriers, creates war and aims to elbow God out of His own world. It can poison other virtues and make other vices more vicious. No wonder William Law said: "Pride must die in us or Christ cannot live in us. ... Look not at pride only as an unbecoming temper, nor at humility only as a decent virtue. ... One is hell, and the other heaven!"

This principle of pride, which is present in the heart of every one of us, if taken to its nth degree is capable of murdering God. If you have difficulty in seeing it in those terms, then consider the cross. One of the purposes of the cross is to make us see plainly what is normally hidden, the foulness and deadly nature of the principle of pride.

In his book *They Met at Calvary*, the late W.E. Sangster wrote, "Jesus Christ was not put to death by a few grossly wicked sins committed by a few monsters of iniquity. He was done to death by an accumulation of ordinary sins, the same sins that you and I have committed and that some of us, maybe, are committing still."

What were those "ordinary sins"? There was the bigotry of the Pharisees. Who hasn't been bigoted? There was the self-seeking of the Sadducees. Who has not been self-seeking? There was the indifference of the crowd. And who has not been indifferent? Add up all the other "ordinary sins" that come to mind, and underlying them you will find pride – the desire to put self-interest before God's interests.

We would never have understood what pride could do until we saw it at the cross. It would never enter our minds that this kind of thing could lead to that kind of situation. But it could, and it did.

"Sin," Dick Keyes reminded us, "is not just conscious hostility toward God; it is also the relegation of God to irrelevance." I doubt whether anyone reading these lines is consciously hostile towards God. But how many of us have relegated Him to irrelevance, giving Him a certain place in our lives, but not the central place? We pay lip service to the fact that Christ is the source of true satisfaction, yet we continue to drink at lukewarm, bacteria-infected wells of our own making because we like to be in control of the water we drink. *That* is relegating God to irrelevance.

Although we are Christians, it is possible to allow our thinking to drift towards the notion that our security, significance and worth depend on our performance, our status, our expertise, our accomplishments. We tend to search for a deeper level of confidence than God, something we can see, something we can touch, rather than the invisible God. God says He is enough. He is the One who can hold us. But we are not sure. So foolishly we step off the Rock onto the shifting sands of self-dependency. And that is the essence of sin.

A second concept we must grasp is this: confession.

CONFESSION

Confession, too, is a word that seems to have slipped out of the modern-day evangelical vocabulary. It is not enough to see the evil nature of sin; we must be willing to admit to it, to confess it. Just as we cannot spell *sin* without the *I*, so the *I* must also be part of confession. Watch how King David personalises his confession in Psalm 32:

> Then I acknowledged my sin to you and did not cover up my iniquity. I said, "I will confess my transgressions to the Lord" – and you forgave the guilt of my sin. (Psa. 32:5)

General confessions that are vague, amorphous and nonspecific are not worth much. One of the characteristics of classic revival is that people begin to confess their sins. The Hebrides Revival began when a young man stood in a prayer meeting and said, "Lord, it is so much humbug when we say *we* have sinned, *our* hands are unclean. *I* have sinned, *my* hands are unclean. Forgive *me*. Oh, forgive *me*."

At that point he broke down in tears, and soon others followed, confessing their sins in the first-person singular. Revival hit the church that night, and a wave of supernatural power followed that has gone down as one of the significant moves of God in the twentieth century.

An old English proverb says, "Confession is good for the soul." "We must own our sin," said an old Puritan, "in order that we may disown it." When we are ready to uncover our sins, then God is ready to cover them.

He who conceals his sins does not prosper, but whoever confesses and renounces them finds mercy. (Prov. 28:13)

C.S. Lewis in *Letters to Malcolm: Chiefly on Prayer* makes the point that when we confess our sin we do more than give God information; we put ourselves on a personal footing with him.

To confess our sin before God is certainly to tell him what he knows much better than we. And also any petition is a kind of telling. We are always completely and therefore equally known to God. That is our destiny whether we like it or not. But though this knowledge never varies the quality of our being known can. We are like earthworms, cabbages, and nebulae, objects of Divine knowledge. But when we assent with all our will to be so known, then we treat ourselves, in relation to God, not as things but as persons. We have unveiled. Not that any veil could have baffled His sight.

The change is in us. The passive changes to the active. Instead of merely being known, we show, we tell, we offer ourselves to view.

To put ourselves on a personal footing with God could, in itself, and without warrant, be nothing but presumption and illusion. But we are taught that it is not; that it is God who gives us that footing. For it is by the Holy Spirit that we cry "Father". By unveiling, by confessing our sin and "making known" our requests, we assume the high rank of persons before Him. And He, descending becomes a person to us. But I should not have said "becomes". In Him there is no becoming. He reveals Himself as Person or reveals that in Him which is a Person. For dare one say it. God is in some measure to a man as that man is to God. The door in God that opens is the door He knocks at.

Nothing is more powerful than Scripture. This wonderful verse found in John's epistle has been both a challenge and a comfort to thousands of Christians:

If we confess our sins, he is faithful and just and will forgive us our sins and purify us from all unrighteousness. (1 John 1:9)

When we bring our sin into the open before God, we must not stop there but go on and repent of it. The uncovering of sin is of little value unless we are prepared to break with it. So from confession we pass to repentance.

REPENTANCE

The Greek word for *repentance* is *metanoia*, meaning "after knowledge" in contradistinction from *pronoia*, which signifies "foreknowledge". Several other states of mind can easily be mistaken for repentance, so before proceeding any further, it may be well to clear away any misunderstandings.

Before considering these states of mind that are superficially similar to repentance, let me draw your attention to this Old Testament verse:

Aaron may bear the iniquity of the holy things. (Exod. 28:38, AV)

The first time I came across this verse, I remember saying to myself, *What an odd phrase. I wonder what it means?* As I studied the context, all became clear.

Old Testament sacrifices provided not only for the plain wickedness of the people but also for the stains that sometimes disfigured holy things. A Jew, for example, was required to tithe his income for the work of God; but the tithe estimate could be faked just like a modern-day tax return. When that was done, it was "an iniquity on holy thing". It was required also of a Jew that he make periodic sacrifices to God, and always it had to be an unblemished lamb, a pair of perfect doves. Theoretically, to use Oswald Chambers's phrase, it had to be "My Utmost for His Highest".

The last book of the Old Testament, Malachi, deals largely with the shabby subterfuges of people who were outwardly religious but grudging in their hearts. And the Aaronic priesthood had as one of its functions to intercede with God not only for the sins of the people but also for their affectations in their holiness.

Repentance is a holy thing. It is the way we deal with our sins and with our wickedness. All serious communication with God begins in repentance. It is the door through which we come into the Christian life, and it is also the door through which we must pass whenever we find ourselves having moved out of relationship with Him.

The church at Ephesus, in Revelation 2, was in trouble with the Lord because they had left their first love. They were commended by Christ because they were orthodox in their doctrine and efficient in their service. But in our Lord's eyes that was not enough. Christ chastises them because they had allowed their love for Him to lapse. "Remember the height from which you have fallen!" says the Saviour to the Ephesian converts. Then He adds: "Repent and do the things you did at first. If you do not repent, I will come to you and remove your lampstand from its place" (Rev. 2:5).

Why does the Saviour encourage them to repent? Had they not done that at the time of their conversion? Of course. But repentance must be seen not only as the entrance into the Christian life; it is also the means by which we improve our Christian life. I have met many Christians who view repentance as a one-time experience, something you do when you are converted and are never expected to do again. That is a fallacy. Repentance is continuous; it is the way we restore our personal relationship with God whenever we find that relationship has been disrupted.

The church at Ephesus, despite their spiritual industriousness, had moved away from a close and intimate relationship with the Lord, and the only way back was through the door of repentance. We cannot hope to restore a close relationship with God unless we understand what it means to repent.

But often our repentance becomes shabby. George Whitfield said, "Our repentance needs to be repented of and our tears washed in the blood of Christ." But what can be wrong with repentance? What about it needs to be washed in the blood of Christ? In order to understand that, consider with me what repentance is not.

It is not regret. Regret is being sorry for oneself, deploring the consequences of one's actions. Archbishop William Temple once asked a candidate for ordination to define *repentance.* The young ordinand answered, "A heart broken because of sin." "Nonsense," replied the archbishop. "Repentance is a heart that has broken away from sin." Repentance is more than regret.

It is not remorse. "Remorse," says one writer, "is sorrow without hope at its heart." One writer provides an illuminating contrast between repentance and remorse in the lives of Peter and Judas. The great Early Church Father Tertullian said that remorse is an emotion of disgust. It eats its heart out instead of seeking a new heart.

In *Why Jesus Never Wrote a Book*, W.E. Sangster explained to his congregation the difference between repentance and remorse by putting it this way:

A youth comes to me in trouble. He has embezzled his employer's money and his employer has found him out. At any time the prosecution will begin. So I go to the employer and plead with him to be merciful, tell him that there are ways in which the money can be restored and the youth can be saved, explain that this is breaking the heart of the boy's good parents, urge him to overlook the thing. And he relents, accepts the money back, and calls the prosecution off. When I have it all tidied up and tell the young man, to my amazement all his distress disappears in a moment. He smiles. He laughs. There is nothing left to worry about. All is well now. He seems to think it was a pity the money had to be paid back. He isn't sorry for his sins at all. He is only sorry for the price he thought he had to pay. There was no real repentance – just remorse – a shabby counterfeit.

Repentance is not reformation. Some people seem to think all that is required is a change of lifestyle for the better, to turn over a new leaf. Amendment is substituted for the atonement. Many try to compensate for some transgression by self-effort, by reforming their character. In the church at Ephesus, before Christ instructed them to return to doing "the things you did at first", He commanded them to repent. Reformation may follow repentance, but it can never precede it.

Repentance is not reparation (making amends). Anyone who, like Zacchaeus, truly repents will, like him, where possible, make amends to the person or persons he or she has wronged. This issue is often overlooked by some spiritual guides dealing with new converts. Scripture talks about producing "fruit in keeping with repentance" (Matt. 3:8). But reparation is one thing, repentance another.

I recall on one occasion teaching on the subject of "gaining a clear conscience" and stressed the need for genuine repentance. For days afterwards people were busy writing letters of apology, making telephone calls to people they had wronged and asking forgiveness for the things they had done. But the actions they took were the consequences, not the cause, of the change that repentance had brought about in them.

If our repentance contains only the elements of regret, remorse and reformation, and if we are sorry not that we have misplaced our dependency but that we have lost our inner peace or found our spirit clouded with guilt, then our repentance is an iniquity on a holy thing.

Having seen what repentance is not, let us now focus on what it is.

WHAT REPENTANCE IS

Repentance literally means "change of mind". A good starting point is to think of it as *a change of mind about where life is found.*

"Repentance," says John White, "is a changed way of looking at things." Writing on this theme in *Changing on the Inside,* he defines *repentance* as the shock that comes from seeing reality. It is a shocking thing to claim to be a Christian and live independently of the life offered to us in Christ, to relegate God to irrelevance. The full realisation of that, brought about by the Holy Spirit, can, says John White, "be like an earthquake in the soul."

C.S. Lewis, when talking about this aspect of repentance, said: "It is just as it was when you passed it before, but your eyes are altered. You see nothing now but realities." And Charles Finney wrote, "To one who truly repents sin looks like a different thing from what it does to him who has not repented."

Another definition of *repentance* I have often used is from Ian Macpherson: "Repentance is a revulsion against sin resulting from a revelation of the righteousness and love of God." A text that comes to mind in this connection is found in Romans 2:4: "God's kindness leads you towards repentance."

When we see how good God is in providing us with all the resources we need to live the life He has designed us to live, any awareness of how we may be ignoring that fact should create a "godly sorrow" that brings repentance (2 Cor 7:10). Some believe repentance is exclusively human. One such proponent put it like this: "I see the folly of my ways, and I make up my mind to change. That is repentance. It begins with me and ends with God."

I prefer to think of repentance as reaching out for something that God initiates. And I think Scripture supports that view. In 2 Timothy 2:25, Paul talks about the necessity for Timothy to instruct those who opposed him "in the hope that God will grant them repentance leading them to a knowledge of the truth". Note the phrase "in the hope that God will *grant* them repentance". Clearly repentance *begins* with God.

This is how I think it works. When I allow myself to focus on the central truth I have been trying to convey in this book, namely that Jesus Christ wants to occupy the central place in my heart, the Holy Spirit stands by, eager and ready to bring me to the place of repentance. It begins by God's giving us some painful insights about ourselves. We grasp something new that we have known before but have never fully seen.

I freely admit there are times (as the history of revival records) when human reluctance to consider one's true spiritual condition seems to be swept away by the Spirit's power and people, deeply convicted of sin, cry out almost against their will. Usually, however, it begins as we supply the willingness and God supplies the power.

In a wonderful moment in C.S. Lewis' *Perelandra*, the hero, Ransom, arrives on the planet Venus to discover that the surface is largely ocean, dotted with floating islands. On one of the islands Ransom meets "the lady", a sort of Eve character who is a strange blend of innocence and curiosity. By some mishap she has been separated from her husband, and in the conversation with Ransom she says:

> I thought that I was carried in the will of Him I love, but now I see I walk with it. I thought that the good things He sent me drew me into them as the waves lift the islands but now I see that it is I who plunge into them with my own legs and arms as when we go swimming.

God wants us to plunge into the waves He sends us. We are not to sit passively but, taking advantage of the grace that flows towards us, respond to what is willed. As Eugene Peterson puts it, "God is already on your case."

Charles Colson has this to say about repentance:

> The repentance God desires of us is not just contrition over particular sins; it is also a daily attitude, a perspective. ... It is the process by which we see ourselves, day by day, as we really are, sinful, needy, dependent people. It is the process by which we see God as He is, awesome majestic holy ... and it so radically alters our perspective that we begin to see the world through God's eyes, not our own. Repentance is the ultimate surrender of the self.

Colson is right. The "ultimate surrender" he refers to is the ongoing submission of our lives into His hands. Whenever we feel ourselves moving away from dependency on Christ and lean on other things, then we must recognise that our misplaced dependency is sin, confess it, and repent of it.

Regular self-assessment is needed. One of the main factors responsible for conviction of sin in our hearts is the Word of God. This is why we should be men and women of the Word who, like the Bereans, "examined the Scriptures every day" (Acts 17:11).

When speaking on this subject a few years ago, I was asked this question, "Doesn't this emphasis on the need for daily repentance lead to a negative view of life?"

My answer was: "Only if you hold within you a concept of God that is negative. If you see God as someone who is interested only in getting you to live right rather than someone who longs to be in a right relationship with you, then repentance will be something you enter into reluctantly rather than freely."

Here is how my friend Scott Hughes put it after having flown from Nashville to the UK to attend a Christ Empowered Living seminar:

> For years I felt condemned by the words "repent for the kingdom of God is at hand". Then I attended your Christ Empowered Living seminar, and everything changed. It taught me that my view of God was coloured by my worldview – not by the truth. If I am honest, I viewed God as someone who was after my obedience and not my friendship. Now I know that true repentance is always positive, because I have a God who is caring and loving. To understand the true meaning of repentance is to understand the true meaning of the Christian life. I learned that repentance is a lifestyle. It's turning towards something that's good – daily. Just as I want to eat daily, I want to repent daily. I find the more I repent, the cleaner I feel inside and the more I want to know God. Quiet times are becoming less of a duty and more of a joy. Now I look forward to hanging out with God. I always knew I had problems, but I never knew how to fix them. I finally learned how when I attended Christ Empowered Living. My entire understanding (mentally and emotionally) of God has taken a 180-degree turn.

WHAT IS INVOLVED IN REPENTANCE?

But how do we go about the task of repenting? Let me go back to another Old Testament passage that depicts well what is involved in repentance.

> *Return, O Israel, to the Lord your God. Your sins have been your downfall. Take words with you and return to the Lord. Say to him: "Forgive all our sins and receive us graciously, that we may offer the fruit of our lips. Assyria cannot save us; we will not mount war-horses. We will never again say, 'Our gods' to what our own hands have made, for in you the fatherless find compassion." (Hos. 14:1–3)*

Let your thoughts go over this important biblical section once again. "Return to the Lord your God; your sins have been your downfall." Sin is best seen as a movement away from God. Any departure from God requires an act of repentance that involves a 180-degree turn in God's direction. A 90-degree turn is not enough. "Repentance," C.S. Lewis said in *Mere Christianity*, is "a movement full speed astern."

"Take words with you and return to the Lord." This means clarifying to yourself and God exactly what you wish to happen. There must be no fumbling of the issue. In my own life I have found a regular need to identify three things that are ever present in my life and need regular repentance: a failure to trust God with my longings, a failure to believe His evaluation of my worth and a failure to see that because He is in my life it has a special meaning and purpose.

"Return to the Lord" underlines the fact once again that true repentance is coming back to God.

"You have stumbled because of your iniquity." We must always be willing to call sin by its rightful name and see it for what it is – iniquity. There must be no euphemisms, no tampering with the labels. To spurn God's grace and rely instead on our own resources is not merely a spiritual infraction; it is iniquitous. And it must be seen as such.

"Receive us graciously, that we may offer the fruit of our lips." The purpose of repentance is that we might worship and live for God in the way He desires – daily dependent on His grace. An animal sacrifice was made to atone for sin, but what God longed for was a sacrifice of praise arising from a realised awareness of forgiveness. Where this is absent – an attitude of thankfulness for sins forgiven – there can be no true worship.

"Assyria cannot save us." Assyria had become an international power during Hosea's time. But for the nation of Israel to look to them when they needed help rather than putting their trust in the living God was, Hosea says, something that must be discountenanced.

"We will not mount war-horses." Israel was expected not to trust in chariots and horses (Psa. 20:7) but in the power and provision of the great El-Shaddai, the Nourisher and Sustainer of His people.

"We will never again say, 'Our gods' to what our own hands have made.'" Their confidence was not to be placed in the works their hands had made. It is one thing to enjoy the things our hands have made; it is another to worship them.

"For in you the fatherless finds compassion." A person who repents stops using his own hands or the works of his hands to gain compassion. Instead, we bring our deepest needs to God and entrust them to Him.

Repentance is a mind-set that looks to God for life, not resting on one's expertise, degrees, academic achievements or business acumen. It is not that we cannot enjoy the fruit of our labours, but we must not live by them. Our lives are hid with Christ in God, so there must be a turning from all self-reliance.

Repentance is turning back to God. Returning to Him for the second or the twenty-second time may be challenging, but there is no other way to profound and positive change. This is how C.S. Lewis defines repentance in *Mere Christianity*:

> Repentance, this willing submission of humiliation and a kind of death, is not something God demands of you before He will take you back and which he could let you off if He chose; it is simply a description of what going back to Him is like. If you ask God to take you back without it you are really asking Him to let you go back without going back. It cannot happen.

Here is a prayer I have used with people many times. Write it into your heart and mind. Pray it now and keep it before you, perhaps in your Bible, and pray it every day. However, before you pray it, let me tell you about Brunner's Law: "The more a decision will affect your life, the more your sinful nature will enter into the debate."

Be aware that other forces are militating against you now. Your carnal nature, the familiarity with which you do this and the forces of darkness want to keep you from surrendering to God. Screwtape, in C.S. Lewis' book, *The Screwtape Letters,* advises a junior devil: "The great thing is to prevent him from doing anything. To think about, to consider it is fine but not to actually do it." Sir Winston Churchill said, "Many people stumble over truth on their way through life, but most get up, dust themselves off, and go on again."

Let nothing detain you. And let there be no deviation. If the Holy Spirit tugs at your heart, pray this prayer with me now.

Heavenly Father, forgive me, I pray, for so foolishly trying to meet my needs in my own way when I see that You and You alone are to be my supply. I repent of my self-sufficiency and self-centredness and ask Your forgiveness for my stubborn and arrogant refusal to trust You with my needs for security, significance and worth. Help me, Lord Jesus, from now on to turn to You in daily dependency and draw from You, the uniquely sufficient God, all I need to hold my life together. In Christ's name. Amen.

Chapter 13

MORE ABOUT
STAYING ON COURSE

Now that we have considered the important issues of the essence of sin and the need for confession and repentance, we are ready to focus on how to bring the three remaining sections of the personality – the mind, the will and the emotions – into correspondence with the divine design.

Attempting to change thinking, set the will in God's direction and manage the emotions without first repenting of misplaced dependency is likely to strengthen self-sufficiency – the very thing we ought to avoid. Some may find this emphasis of dependency on God for life to work and work effectively to be disturbing. Some say such teaching tends to sap human potential and weaken human resolve. Scripture makes clear that we cannot be at our best unless we are at our best in Christ. We were made by Him and for Him, says Paul in his letter to the Colossians, and it follows that we cannot function effectively without His leadership in our lives.

> *For by him all things were created: things in heaven and on earth, visible and invisible, whether thrones or powers or rulers or authorities; all things were created by him and for him.* (Col. 1:16)

Far from weakening personality, the indwelling Christ strengthens it. No one would deny that the apostle Paul was a gifted man with a keen and comprehensive mind. He was born into the intellectual aristocracy of the Jews but enjoyed the distinction of being a Roman citizen, thus having access to the classical learning of that ancient culture.

He declared on one occasion that he was "faultless" before the law (Phil. 3:6). Yet he struggled within. He had no constant victory over his thoughts, and though he did not allow wrong thoughts to become deeds, he could not help identifying with them.

Nor was he any more victorious in relation to his will. He would decide not to do a certain thing, and then do it. "I do not understand what I do," he said when writing to the Romans. "For what I want to do I do not do, but what I hate I do" (Rom. 7:15).

He discovered on the Damascus road that not only was Christ alive but He was willing to live in the lives of those who would give themselves to Him. He discovered, too, that though he was not instantly made perfect and temptations would still assault, he was strong in the power and strength of Christ. In relation to his will, he did the things his Lord wanted him to do. In fact, it would be true to say they did them together. "I can do everything," he said, "through him who gives me strength" (Phil. 4:13).

Paul never ceased to wonder at the fact that Christ was living in him, empowering him and motivating him towards a life that he had never imagined possible. Previously he had constantly struggled in his thinking, feeling and willing; now there was steady success. He was strong in the strength of his resident Lord.

Consider this: In the thirteen letters Paul wrote, one phrase is repeated over and over again – "in Christ". Adolf Deissmann, the German scholar, has counted the number of times Paul uses this and similar expressions and found they total 164. How important it seemed to Paul that he was in Christ and that Christ was in him. It seemed to be the pivotal point around which he constructed all his writings.

The victorious life, the empowered life, is the life lived in Christ. When He is at the centre of our being – thinking, willing and feeling in our responsive hearts – then we begin to experience the kind of life God intended for us in the beginning. How do we allow Christ to be at the centre of our thinking, our willing and our feelings?

We begin with the mind. The mind plays a great part in human functioning. Some would say a primal part. "As he thinks in his heart," says Scripture, "so is he" (Prov. 23:7, NKJV). With the imagination – so powerful a segment of the mind – the will is strongly shaped and influenced. Even when we think our physical appetites are ruling, it is often because the mind has coaxed the carnal side of our nature and permitted it.

HAVING THE MIND OF CHRIST

No wonder the apostle Paul insisted, "Let this mind be in you which was also in Christ Jesus" (Phil. 2:5, NKJV). From the mind of Christ, all good things come. We must learn how to receive the mind of Christ. It will not be easy. The thought forms that we have developed over the years will not be broken without some work and commitment on our part. But given our consent and co-operation, Christ is able to renew our minds and impart His mind to us. Put nothing beyond the power of His grace. Nothing.

The Bible has a great deal to say about the mind. The words *mind, thoughts, think* and *thinking* are found in Scripture more than three hundred times. God views the mind as an important part of human functioning.

All thinking takes place by putting words together in a way that makes up sentences. So, in fact, when we *think*, we are really talking to ourselves. Psychologists call this our inner monologue. And from our inner conversations come our feelings and our reactions, which in turn affect our behaviour.

Much of our thinking takes place unconsciously. Mostly we are aware of what we are thinking, but our thinking goes on even when we are not aware of it. How many times have you been asked what you were thinking and answered, "Oh, I don't know." Some believe we are influenced as much by our unconscious thoughts as those of which we are cognisant.

Thoughts also run through our minds at a tremendous rate. Don Dulaney, a social psychologist, says thoughts go through our minds at the rate of 1,300 words a minute. That's a high rate of thinking. I often illustrate this when teaching by writing words on the overhead projector or blackboard such as these: dentist, bounced cheque, submission, redundancy, etc.

Then I ask how people are reacting to some of these words. Sometimes one word or phrase – like *bounced cheque*, for example – can cause sentences like this to speed through our minds: *Oh dear, that cheque I gave has bounced. What will they think of me? How can I face them? What can I do to make amends?* One word can trigger a whole train of sentences.

To win the battle of the mind is to win in one of the greatest areas of life. When the Bible says, "You will keep in perfect peace him whose mind is steadfast, because he trusts in you" (Isa. 26:3), we know at once that the operative phrase is "because he trusts in you".

Nothing is more rewarding than having a mind that is stayed on God. In the minds of far too many Christians, the old muddled, soiled and fearful thinking continues. The "traffic still runs on the old habit tracks", as some-one has put it, and far too many believers have an "underworld" life on which professed allegiance to Christ seems to have no effect at all.

"Our minds, naturally speaking," says the New Testament scholar Douglas Moo, "are stuck in a rut, a pattern of thinking that is antagonistic to the will of God. Successful Christian living depends on getting out of that rut and establishing another one that is characterised by biblical values and ways of thinking."

Nothing can be clearer in Scripture than that our minds need to be changed. One of my favourite Bible translations is the J.B. Phillips version. I think his rendering of Romans 12:2 has not been surpassed by any modern translation:

> *Don't let the world around you squeeze you into its own mould, but let God remould your minds from within, so that you may prove in practice that the plan of God for you is good, meets all his demands and moves towards the goal of true maturity.*

A great deal of emphasis in today's counselling community (both Christian and non-Christian) is on "cognitive restructuring", the process of changing wrong thinking to right thinking. It is said that no real change can take place until a person's thinking is changed. With that, Scripture would appear to agree. Take these texts for example:

> *Finally, brothers, whatever is true, whatever is noble, whatever is right, whatever is pure, whatever is lovely, whatever is admirable – if anything is excellent or praiseworthy – think about such things.* (Phil. 4:8)

The mind of sinful man is death, but the mind controlled by the Spirit is life and peace. (Rom. 8:6)

We demolish arguments and every pretension that sets itself up against the knowledge of God, and we take captive every thought to make it obedient to Christ. (2 Cor. 10:5)

Set your minds on things above, not on earthly things. (Col. 3:2)

Why do our minds need to be changed? Why is it necessary, as J.B. Phillips put it, to have our minds remoulded from within? Because since the Fall, much of our thinking is based on untruths. Chris Thurman in *The Lies We Tell Ourselves* says the real problems of the mind arise from the lies we tell ourselves.

He says:

Your brain is like a tape deck. It can both record and play back, and it has access to a personal library of thousands of tapes ready to play at a moment's notice. These tapes hold all the beliefs, attitudes and expectations that you have "recorded" during your life. Some of the tapes inside your brain are truthful, such as "You can't please everybody" or "You reap what you sow." Some of these tapes are lies, such as "Things have to go my way for me to be happy," or "It is easier to avoid problems than face them." Many tapes lie in your mind without your even knowing it. They play unconsciously when life presses the "Play" button through some kind of circumstance.

Many Christian counsellors, who follow the cognitive restructuring model, teach people how to identify the wrong things they are telling themselves and challenge them to replace them with truths that are in harmony with God's Word.

IT'S AS EASY AS ABC

A simple formula is followed, called the ABC Theory of Emotion, first developed by the psychologist Albert Ellis and outlined in this form:

A represents any event or circumstance.
B represents our evaluation of the event or circumstance.
C represents the consequent emotion.

Just as when reading the alphabet you do not go from A to C without passing through B, so the theory says that any event or circumstance (A) is powerless in itself to produce an emotional response (C) until it has been evaluated. In other words, A does not produce C; it has to pass through B. Let's illustrate with a practical example:

A (situation)   Minister whose church is
                                 not growing.

| B | (evaluation) | I am a worthless person. |
| C | (consequent emotion) | Low mood, perhaps even depression. |

The situation in which the minister finds himself is not what causes his low mood or depression, because *A* does not control *C*. What is causing his low spirits is what he is telling himself about the situation. He could tell himself something like this: "My church is not growing, and I am deeply concerned about this. I must analyse the situation and seek the advice of my peers." He would feel some concern, perhaps even sadness, but not the debilitating and incapacitating feelings of depression. The depression arises because of the lie he is telling himself: "I am a worthless person."

Cognitive restructuring would focus on changing the *B* in this situation and showing the depressed minister that his low mood comes from the lie he is foolishly telling himself. A church not growing may, perhaps should, cause a minister some concern, but it has nothing to do with his worth as a person.

Some Christian therapists add the letters *D* and *E* to Ellis's formula.

| D | (dispute) | represents confronting and challenging the perceived lie. |
| E | (exchange) | represents replacing the lie with a verse of Scripture or a truth more in harmony with God's Word. |

Care must be taken not to dispute the emotion and pretend that you do not feel the way you do. That is dishonest. It is the thought underlying the emotion that has to be disputed.

In the example quoted above, the minister would be encouraged to challenge his wrong belief, "I am a worthless person", and perhaps replace it with "My worth in Christ is unimpeachable. I am valued by Him not because of what I do but who I am in Him." This might be reinforced with a text from Scripture such as Luke 12:7 or Ephesians 1:3–9.

THREE IMPORTANT CAVEATS

I have no difficulty with the ABC Theory of Behaviour, and I have often used it when counselling. I would, however, like to make three suggestions.

First, any attempt to change the thinking must follow, not precede, the issue of misplaced dependency. Unless we approach the concept of cognitive restructuring from the position of deep dependency on Christ, we are likely to depend more on our ability to change our thoughts than on Him.

Second, the truths contained in God's Word require the ministry of the Holy Spirit in order for them to lodge deeply in the mind. This is done through meditation in the Scriptures. Bible meditation is a lost art among many modern-day believers. Thoughts cannot just be fitted into the mind the way we put tapes in a tape deck. Because of sin, the mind resists and such resistance must be overcome through patient and persistent application of God's Word to the mind.

If all this sounds like work to those who say, "We have only to believe and all things are possible," then I can offer no argument. Of course it is work. The Christian life is more than just believing; it is also receiving. I have met many Christians whose creed is "only believe". Then I have sat with them in the counselling room and have had to point out that "only believing" has apparently not drawn the life of God into their souls. In many who adopted this position it was obvious that love did not burn in them, joy did not flow from them and peace did not shine through them.

The life of God is not to be had on the cheap. It cost Him a cross and it will cost us something as well, more than singing a few songs. It is not salvation by works I am advocating here but the discipline of devotion that seeks to know God more intimately. It is the discipline of receiving and doing. Wrong habits of thinking are not broken in a moment. It is easy for a ship to change its flag but keep its course. It will need work. He will give you His mind if you are prepared to give Him yours.

Third, no real change can come about until we recognise the mind's core unbelief. The lie that stains all lies – "You can be a more fulfilled person by acting independently of Christ" – must be disputed or there can be no true mind change.

On many occasions I have counselled people who have been through a course of cognitive restructuring and appeared to be greatly helped, yet they still struggled with deep problems in their personalities. Upon investigation I discovered that often the cause was not that they failed to repent of misplaced dependency, but they were busy changing what I call "surface lies". The lie "that stains all other lies" was still playing like background music in their personalities. Only when that lie is challenged and changed can spiritual health come to the soul and Christ be master of our minds.

Let this mind be in you which was also in Christ Jesus. (Phil. 2:5, NKJV)

MASTER OF THE WILL

It is not enough that Christ be master of our minds; He must also be master of our wills. Because the will is greatly influenced by the mind, whatever we believe will bring us what we long for – a relationship in which we find security, self-worth and significance – the will is then set in the direction of reaching that goal. If our minds have a clear understanding where true life is found, then our goal will be to know more of Christ. If our minds are muddled on this issue, then the goals we pursue will be foolish and idolatrous.

Because He respects our freedom of choice, God will allow us to chase empty idols and false images for the rest of our lives – if that is what we want.

Ron Mehl puts it like this in *Ten(der) Commandments:*

He will allow you to dig your own cistern, to pick up your shovel and scrape away at the rocky soil through the days and weary years until your hands bleed and you are worn away by your useless toil. If you insist on it he will let you have your way. But you will have to walk right past His arms to do it.

The Church of Jesus Christ has within its ranks multiplied thousands of Christian idolaters – people who profess to be Christ's followers but believe deep down that in order to experience wholeness they need something other than Christ.

That "something" then becomes their goal. Keep in mind the definition of a *goal* in this context: A goal is an objective we pursue because we believe that is where life is to be found. And any goal that we pursue, believing that is where life is found, is an idol.

Sometimes when counselling I would say to someone, "Finish this sentence: For me to live is ..." If the person was a Christian, with some familiarity of the Scriptures, he or she would respond immediately, "For me to live is Christ." "Yes," I would say, "that is the required response, but let's look now at the real response. This time be absolutely open and honest. Are you saying that you draw your life wholly from Christ or from some other source?" More often that approach would lead to some powerful counselling sessions as people began to realise their life was found not in Christ but in the pursuit of a chosen goal that was outside Him.

I remember one occasion when I put that question to a man who responded in these words: "For me to live is ... control."

"Can you say a little more about that?" I asked. "Unless everything is under my control," he said, "then great fear and anxiety arise within me, to the extent that sometimes I am almost incapacitated by them."

If I were sitting with you right now and asked you to finish the sentence, "For me to live ..." what would you say?

In the following conversation a young man, a Christian, working in an office in London, has a frank and relaxed exchange with his employer, a high-flying lawyer, Ms G. The employer claims she is not religious, at which point the young man says:

"Look, you do have a religion and I think you're deeply religious. Shall I tell you what your religion is?"

"The law?"

"No, no, that's just the means you've chosen to achieve your ends. Your religion, Ms. G, is Order."

"Order?"

"Yes, that's the god you worship. That's what your life is all about. You live in a chaotic jungle, the financial killing fields of the City of London, but your whole life is dedicated to bringing Order out of chaos. ... Your devotion to Order is the first thing I noticed about you. Your appearance is immaculate. No hair is ever out of place. No skirt is ever creased. Your filing systems are things of rational, logical beauty. Your reports, your memoranda, your letters all shine with the most well-ordered intelligence. Your clients find you indestructibly well-organised and utterly in control – and that's what it's all about isn't it? And how do you reduce chaos to order? You exercise your reason, your logic and your intelligence to make an enormous success of your profession. Money, power and status combine to give you a lot of control over your life and the more control you have the easier it is for you to luxuriate in Order – to commune regularly with your god. Ah yes, Ms. G, never doubt you're deeply religious!

You go to worship every day for hours on end at your office, your Holy Trinity is money, power and status, and over and above your trinity is the godhead, Order, the ground of your being, the fount of all goodness, your raison d'être, your love, your life."

Ms G, in order to hold her world together, needed order. That was her functional god. What's yours? I referred earlier to David Powlinson's use of the term "functional gods". When we pursue something other than the true God because we foolishly believe that is where we can find life, that something becomes "god" to us.

Often the things we are pursuing are not in themselves wrong. Nothing is wrong, for example, in pursuing a good education, gaining a degree or several degrees, improving your financial position or climbing up the career ladder, but if those things become for us the route to life, then we must not be surprised to hear the Lord say to us, as He did to the ancient Israelites, "My people have committed two sins: They have forsaken me, the spring of living water, and have dug their own cisterns, broken cisterns that cannot hold water" (Jer. 2:13).

Here is another helpful quotation from David Powlinson in the *Journal of Biblical Counseling*:

As a Christian you profess that God controls all things and works everything to His glory and your ultimate well being. You profess that God is your rock and refuge, a very present help in whatever troubles you face. You profess to worship Him, trust Him, love Him, obey Him. But in that moment – hour, day, season of anxiety, you live as if you needed to control things. You live as if money or someone else's approval, or a "successful" sermon, or your grade on an exam, or good health, or avoiding conflict, or getting your way, or ... matters more than trusting and loving God. You live as if some temporary good feeling could provide you refuge, as if your actions could make the world right. Your functional god competes with your professed God.

How do we ensure that we have no "functional gods" in our lives? By making the simple decision to have one overarching goal that brings all other lesser goals into their right perspective. The apostle Paul gives us the secret of doing this in the following passage:

> So we make it our goal to please him, whether we are at home in the body or away from it. For we must all appear before the judgment seat of Christ, that each one may receive what is due to him for the things done while in the body, whether good or bad. (2 Cor. 5:9–10)

Paul's goal in life was this – *to please Christ*. That goal was not uncertain, could not be undermined, and because Christ was at work empowering him, it was not unreachable. Ah, but you might say, "Paul was a spiritual genius. He had experiences ordinary Christians do not have." It is true that he had unusual visions and revelations, but when he wrote those words to the

Corinthians, you may be sure they were for all Christians, throughout the whole of time.

So if you have not already done so, do it now. Based on the biblical belief that only Christ can give you what your soul aches for, set your will in the direction of pleasing Him. Make a choice that determines every other choice. When your overall goal is to please the Lord in every situation, then whoever you are – a businessman or businesswoman, a teacher, a student, a homemaker, an office worker, a musician, a singer or a minister – all you need to do when facing a challenging or difficult situation is to say, "What must I do to please the Lord in this?"

When you attempt to please the Lord in every situation, you are pursuing a goal that carries with it the guarantee of divine empowerment. This must not be taken to mean that you will never experience any negative emotions, but you will not be disabled by them. Disabling emotions are indicators that we are pursuing wrong goals. Behind most problems ever brought to me in counselling is a goal that has either been blocked, is uncertain or is unreachable.

This naturally leads to a consideration of the last section of the personality – the emotions. How do we go about dealing with our emotions so that we are in charge of them and not the other way around.

We have already discussed the phrase used by Kevin Huggins, "Signal Emotions," and the concept that negative feelings are like the red light that appears on the dashboard of the car when there is a problem. Here's what another author, Chris Thurman, has to say about this in *The Lies We Tell Ourselves*:

I find it rather amazing that an inanimate object such as an automobile can sometimes appear to have more common sense than a human being. If you purchase a brand new car, it will have several computerized check systems built into it. If your car's oil level gets too low, a red warning light will flash on the dashboard. The same happens when the antifreeze, gasoline and brake and transmission fluids get low. The car senses a problem approaching, so it sends a warning signal for something to be done. If the warning is heeded, the car's life is extended many extra miles. If not the car breaks down prematurely.

MANAGING THE EMOTIONS

Something similar happens to us when our goals become blocked. Problem emotions signal that some maintenance work is needed. We need to look at what is going on inside us.

Here are a few suggestions I have found helpful for dealing with problem emotions. First, face and feel your emotions. Don't pretend they are not there. Christians struggle with this issue more than non-Christians. This is because Christian teaching says we should put away things like anger, lust and malice (Col. 3:5–10). And whenever we experience these feelings, because we wish they were not there, we can so easily deny their presence.

One secular psychologist refers to Christians in general as suffering from ecclesiogenic neurosis. The word *ecclesia* is the Greek word for *church*. The word *neurosis* needs no explanation. "Most Christians I have known," he says, "deal with unacceptable emotions by denying they are there." Is he right? My experience says there is enough truth in what he says to make me feel uncomfortable.

An interesting book that argues for an honest approach to emotions is *Emotional Intelligence* by Daniel Goleman. He says that people who are unwilling to face their emotions are not good at building relationships.

He claims that EQ (emotional quotient) is more important than IQ (intelligence quotient) and says that IQ takes second position to EQ in determining outstanding job performance. What Goleman is talking about is maturity. We are as mature as our ability to handle our emotions.

Simply bringing feelings into awareness can have beneficial effects. A study at Southern Methodist University in the USA took 63 laid-off managers who were understandably angry. The researchers said to half the group, "We want you to keep a journal for five days, spending twenty minutes writing out your deepest feelings and reflections on what you are going through." The other half were not given any instructions except to deal with their emotions the best they could. Those who kept journals found new jobs faster than those who didn't.

The more aware we are of our feelings, the sooner we recover from them. Awareness is a key issue. You can't begin to deal with any negative emotion unless you first admit that it is there. When an emotion arises, don't attempt to deny it or pretend it is not there. Face it and feel it. Any emotion that is denied, you will have to pay in compound interest at some later stage in your life. And why? Simply because emotions leak; they can literally affect physical functioning and give you a pain in the neck.

Second, discover how they arose. Whenever a problem emotion arises in your life – anxiety and fear, guilt and shame, anger and resentment – ask yourself such questions as these: "What is the possible goal that is being thwarted in my life at this time? What is the actual block to that goal?" If it is something outside yourself (such as a person or set of circumstances), the likelihood is, you will feel anger or resentment. Whatever your goal is, something is thwarting it.

If it is something inside you – a fear of failure for example – then your goal is probably uncertain. Your goal is reachable in the sense – you have the ability to reach it, but you are afraid you might not get to it. And getting to it probably means you are depending more on that than on Christ to make your life work.

If the emotions are guilt and shame, then your goal is no doubt an unreachable one. You are striving for the unattainable and, because that is where you see life, the frustration of not getting to it causes you to come down upon yourself in self-denigration. Self-inflicted guilt is often a device we use to browbeat ourselves.

When Mike Tyson became angry and bit off a chunk of Evander Holyfield's ear during their 1997 heavyweight boxing title match, it cost him 3 million dollars and a year's suspension from boxing. Boxing experts think it was because Holyfield had head-butted Tyson when they fought seven months earlier, a match Tyson also lost. You and I know a little more. It happened because of a goal that was being blocked.

I came across this in an article in *Fast Company*. It told the tale of Bill Gates' tirade.

> Bill Gates ... eyes are bulging and his oversized glasses are askew. His face is flushed and spit is flying from his mouth. He's in a small crowded conference room at the Microsoft campus with 20 young Microsofties gathered around an oblong table. Most look at their chairman with outright fear, if they look at him at all. The sour smell of terror fills the room. While Gates continues his angry tirade the hapless programmers fumble and stutter, trying to persuade or at least placate him. All to no avail. No one seems to be able to get through – except a small soft spoken Chinese-American woman who seems to be the only person in the room who is unfazed by his tantrum. She looks him in the eye while everyone else avoids eye contact. Twice she interrupts his tirade to address him in quiet tones. The first time her words seem to calm him a bit before his shouting continues. The second time he listens in silence thoughtfully gazing down at the table. Then his anger suddenly vanishes and he tells her, "Okay – this looks good. Go ahead." With that he ends the meeting.

This woman's unflappability is a skill of self-control, overcoming her anxiety in the situation. I do not know if that woman was a Christian, but she did display a quality that resembles a fruit of the Spirit that the apostle Paul talks about in Galatians 5: self-control. All Christians have access to this as well as to the other eight, and they are more than natural abilities – they are supernaturally endowed by the Holy Spirit. They are the nine marks of God's presence in a life committed to Him. Here is the full list: love, joy, peace, patience, kindness, goodness, faithfulness, gentleness, and self-control (Gal. 5:22–23).

Wise Christians understand that negative emotions tell them something about themselves. They allow their emotions to alert them to the need for some fundamental changes in what they are pursuing.

Third, decide to express emotions in harmony with biblical principles. This does not mean giving free reign to feelings, "letting it all hang out". Maturity means managing those feelings so that they are expressed appropriately.

"The mind," says John Stott, "is meant to stand as censor over the emotions." That applies also to the will. We can choose how we express our emotions, in carnal ways or godly ways. If someone has hurt you and because of it you feel angry, always remember you have a choice as to how you express the emotion. You can respond biblically or carnally. You can blow your top or, using the resources of Jesus Christ that are available to us every moment of our lives, you can pause to ask yourself, "Am I feeling this way because of some goal that is being blocked?" If the answer is yes, use the moment as a brief time of introspection to see what is causing the negative response.

There are four ways to deal with negative emotions:

1. Express them – blow your top.
2. Suppress them – keep the lid on them.
3. Repress them – deposit them in the depths of the unconscious.
4. Confess them – admit to them but keep them in control.

There is no doubt in my mind which is the more excellent way. We must confess them to ourselves, admit that we have them and acknowledge them in a way that is powerful.

While I was teaching this in Singapore some years ago, a woman said, "But it is our culture to mask our emotions. If we get in touch with them, aren't we going against our culture?"

"If your culture does not contribute to good emotional health," I said, "then choose health."

Let no one think, however, that strong emotions cannot be controlled. John Stott asks, "What should we say to a married man who has fallen in love with another woman? That he cannot help himself? That this is the real thing and that he must divorce his wife? No, we say this: Wait a minute. You are not the helpless victim of your emotions. You have accepted a lifelong commitment to your wife. You have God's promise of help in this. Draw on it."

Emotions may influence us, but they should not rule us. Staying on course depends on how well we manage these five areas of our personality. But is life just about personal management, or is it something more? That is the thought that must occupy us in the next and last chapter.

Chapter 14

HOW THEN SHALL WE LIVE?

There is a lot more to Christian living than just overcoming problems.

It is not wrong to explore why we do the things we do and ponder the motivations that direct so much of our lives, but there is something deeply selfish in the engrossing concern to live above circumstances – and nothing more.

So what more is there to living than a life of overcoming problems? Its purpose is to please the One who has put within us His endless life. And that life, as shown by Jesus, is a life of loving service and limitless sacrifice.

When God comes into a human life, He also seeks to get out. God's life will never be blocked. He comes into our heart *so that He might pass through it in blessing to others*. And where it cannot pass through, it cannot fully enter.

Often, as a pastor and a counsellor, I have been asked, "What is God's overall purpose for our lives as Christians?" My reply has always been *relationships*. May I remind you of the extraordinary statement of D. Broughton Knox that caused such a paradigm shift in my life:

> We learn from the Trinity that relationship is the essence of reality and therefore the essence of our existence ... and we also learn that the way this relationship should be expressed is by concern for others.

We were built by our Creator to relate in the same way God relates, with other-centredness. Men and women cannot function effectively or rise to their highest potential unless they are in a loving relationship with God and then seek to reflect that love to others.

ALL RELATIONSHIPS AFFECTED BY THE FALL

The Fall corrupted both vertical and horizontal relationships. The original sin affected Adam's relationship with God and also with Eve; she also changed in her relationship with God and the way she related to her husband. From then on relationships have been fraught with problems; they became self-centred rather than other-centred.

This is what Jeremiah said centuries later about the kind of relationships that can be expected because of the Fall:

"Beware of your friends; do not trust your brothers. For every brother is a deceiver, and every friend a slanderer. Friend deceives friend, and no-one speaks the truth. They have taught their tongues to lie; they weary themselves with sinning. You live in the midst of deception; in their deceit they refuse to acknowledge me," declares the Lord. (Jer. 9:4–6)

And King Solomon implied that few would find continuously fulfilled relationships.

Many a man claims to have unfailing love, but a faithful man who can find? (Prov. 20:6)

The quality of relationships here on earth is affected to a great degree by the sinful nature that continues to plague us until death. One of the reasons Christ came was to reverse the effects of the Fall by bringing men and women into such a close relationship with Himself that the same other-centred energy that flows through Him might be at work in them.

"To live is to love," said Augustine. This statement beautifully sums up the life of our Lord. His whole life was one of obedience to the Father's will and limitless sacrifice. From the time He first came to realise that He was the Son of God to the moment He gave His last expiring cry on the cross, His whole life was spent in serving others.

Peter summarised the Saviour's life in this way:

You know what has happened throughout Judea, beginning in Galilee after the baptism that John preached

— how God anointed Jesus of Nazareth with the Holy Spirit and power, and how he went around doing good and healing all who were under the power of the devil, because God was with him. (Acts 10:37–38)

Jesus was entirely selfless.

THE MOST UNSELFISH MAN WHO EVER WALKED THE EARTH

Comb the record of His days here on earth and you will not find one self-centred incident. Take His last hours. Study His demeanour from the traitorous kiss of Judas until His last moments on the cross, and His thoughts are always for others. His silence in the judgment hall is explained in part by the high priest's question about His disciples. He was determined to say nothing about them. In the garden He hastened to identify Himself to the officers in charge of the soldiers so that His disciples could get away quickly. "If you are looking for me, then let these men go" (John 18:4–8). Always, he was other-centred.

After leaving the high priest's palace, He turned to Peter and with a look unsealed a fount of tears as Peter went out and wept bitterly. What was it about that look that turned Simon Peter to tears? Was it a look of contempt? No. Derision? No. Resentment? No. I believe it was a look that showed hurt but no rejection.

If you have ever looked into the face of someone you have hurt but saw no rejection in their eyes, then you will have seen something of the expression that must have been on the countenance of Christ that morning when on His way to the house of the high priest to be tried, He turned and looked upon the disaffected Peter. Only He could have known what those eyes of Jesus were saying to him. "I warned you, Peter, yet I love you still."

On the road to the cross, our Lord thought so little of Himself that He paused to speak to the weeping women. And when the crucifying hammers swung through the air, driving the iron nails into His hands, His prayer was not for Himself but for others. He did not say, "Are these the brutes for whom I am dying?" No. He prayed, "Father, forgive them; for they know not what they do" (Luke 23:34, AV).

When the cross is lifted up and dropped with a thud into its socket, He is concerned with others still. He comforts the penitent thief and makes provision for His desolate mother. And when He is aware that sin's penalty has been paid, He cries with a loud voice: "It is finished." And finished it was. Sin was overcome, death vanquished, heaven opened. God revealed.

How sad that we who follow the One whose life was one of limitless service to others are so often preoccupied with ourselves. Me. Me. Me. Our Lord's mind was not preoccupied with Himself but with how He could bring His Father's love to the men and women who crossed His path. No wonder E. Stanley Jones said, "Christianity is the science of relating well to others in the spirit of Jesus Christ."

OUR LORD'S ANSWER TO A
PROBING QUESTION

Jesus made clear the purpose of living when in answer to a lawyer's question – "What is the greatest commandment?" – He quoted with approval the Hebrew law:

> "Love the Lord your God with all your heart and with all your soul and with all your mind." This is the first and greatest commandment. And the second is like it: "Love your neighbour as yourself." All the Law and the Prophets hang on these two commandments. (Matt. 22:37–40)

No Christian will have difficulty understanding this statement: "You shall love the Lord your God with all your heart", but many are confused by our Lord's next words, "Love your neighbour as yourself". Based on a misunderstanding of these words, some teach that before you can love others you must learn to love yourself.

I know some who instruct people that the proper order in relationships is this:

1. God
2. Yourself
3. Others

I quote from a church-based manual on the theme of "Relationships" that says: "After God you must put yourself next, you must learn to love yourself because unless you do you will never be able to love others in the way you should." People in this church are encouraged to get together in groups for the purpose of learning to love themselves and then go out and love others.

Now I readily admit that some do not love themselves. They have been so badly damaged in their developmental years that they have chosen to adopt an attitude of self-hate. Such people, however, are more the exception than the rule. Jesus is referring here to the attitude found in the hearts of all normal men and women – the attitude of self-concern and self-love.

Our Lord's words spoken to the inquiring lawyer must be seen not simply as a statement but as a command. Christ is making the point that generally speaking we all have a natural love for ourselves and a concern for our own survival and welfare. We all like to have a good home, a happy family and good health. Jesus' point is that we ought also to seek that for others.

John Stott put it like this in *Authentic Christianity*:

> Do you not like to satisfy your hunger? Then you must with similar urgency feed your neighbour. Jesus is presupposing not commanding love. We desire and seek what we think is for our own good and this universal trait becomes the rule by which all loving self sacrifice must be measured.

Self-love is quite different from love of self. Scripture recognises the legitimacy of self-love, just as long as it is not love *only* for the self, not sought for its own sake and never divorced from the equal love of others. Love of self is where a person is preoccupied with self, entirely self-centred, perhaps even narcissistic. This kind of love is condemned everywhere in Scripture.

The purpose of living, then, is loving involvement with God and loving involvement with others. That is the true purpose of image bearers. We are to love God and love others, with the same love by which we are loved.

This is a moment for complete candour. Each one of us must ask ourselves, "How well do I relate, first to God and then to others?" If you are anything like me, I imagine you will be challenged more by this question than any other.

Almost every problem we struggle with in life, other than a purely physical problem, will have something to do with relationships. Many counsellors will tell you that almost every problem brought to them has a relational component. If we close our heart to relationships, we close our hearts to God. It is as simple as that.

WHAT IS CHRISTIANITY?

It is impossible to give a definitive description of Christianity without bringing into it the thought of relationships. A few years ago I read a report of a group of Christians in one of Britain's universities who wanted to share with their non-Christian friends and colleagues what Christianity was all about. They booked one of the university's rooms and printed and distributed hundreds of leaflets with these words:

What Is Christianity?

Hear five of your colleagues share the
result of their research into this
2,000-year-old phenomenon!

The leaflets gave the time, date and location of the
meeting and indicated that each speaker would take just
five minutes to share the results of their research. On the
night, several hundred students turned up.

The first speaker began by saying that Christianity
is a set of beliefs. To be a Christian, he explained,
requires a confident belief in the fact that Jesus Christ
came into this world from the Father, lived a sinless
life, was crucified, rose again, returned to the Father
and will one day come again to this world to usher in
His kingdom.

The second speaker said that Christianity is not just a
set of beliefs but also a creed to live by. What is believed,
he said, must work itself out in behaviour. But the
behaviour of a true Christian, he pointed out, is not the
result of self-effort but surrender to the Person of Christ
so that He is able to live His life through those
committed to Him. "Jesus, in His Sermon on the
Mount," he said, "was not saying, 'live like this and you
will become a Christian,' but, 'become a Christian and
you will live like this.'" A good point.

The third speaker said that Christianity is all the other
two speakers had said but also this – a sacramental
fellowship. The central rite of the Christian religion, he
pointed out, is a simple meal of bread and wine with
different denominations using differing descriptions:
Holy Communion, the Lord's Table, the Lord's Supper,

the Eucharist, Mass and so on. This simple meal, he explained, was celebrated regularly by Christians of all denominations so that they would never forget the sacrifice made by Christ for them on the cross.

The fourth speaker rose to make the point that Christianity was also a rescue mission. "The genius of the gospel," he explained, "is not about refreshing the parts that other religions may fail to reach, but saving men and women from hell." He went on to make the point that hell was not a popular doctrine but was something Jesus, the founder of Christianity, constantly warned His hearers about. He finished by making the point that hell may be left out of many modern-day pulpits, but it is certainly an important part of the Bible's teaching.

The fifth and final speaker defined Christianity as "an escalator to heaven". "It is not only about rescuing us from hell," he said, "but to bring us at last to heaven." He went on to say that it is not God's purpose to save His children, then leave them lying around somewhere. They are saved *from* hell and saved *for* heaven.

Now all of these definitions, of course, were entirely accurate; and following the presentation, a number of students stayed behind and made decisions for Jesus Christ. However, in my view, despite the commendable definitions and descriptions given, they missed the very heart of the Christian faith – relationships. The idea of relationships was implied in some of the things they said, but relationships are such an integral part of Christianity that without them it cannot be defined.

SCRIPTURE – A BOOK ABOUT RELATIONSHIPS

Scripture speaks about relationships with great clarity. We made the point earlier that Christianity, in fact, began in a relationship. Mark's Gospel says: "He appointed twelve – designating them apostles – that they might be with him and that he might send them out to preach" (Mark 3:14). Note the words, "that they might be with him". The first part of their calling was not to preach but "to be with him" – relationships.

Take another verse:

Make every effort to keep the unity of the Spirit through the bond of peace. (Eph. 4:3)

Scripture recognises that good human relationships are not easy to manage or maintain, so it encourages us to put some effort into the task.

Be devoted to one another in brotherly love. Honour one another above yourselves. (Rom. 12:10)

The term *one another* occurs more than fifty times in the New Testament. The text encourages us to be *devoted* to one another – not to put up with one another, or tolerate one another, but to relate to one another in the same way that we relate to Jesus Christ – devotedly.

Therefore confess your sins to each other and pray for each other so that you may be healed. (James 5:16)

Do you know of a church where this scripture is practised? I have not come across one in the fifty years of my ministry. It tells us that we are to be open with one another, trust one another with the deepest issues of our lives, even confessing our sins to one another. One man said to me, "If I was to confess my sins to anyone in my church, I can guarantee it would be all over the community by the next day." See how far off-track we are in the area of relationships?

Sometimes when conducting a Christ Empowered Living seminar, I have asked the audience if they can recite for me John 3:16. Most people, I find, know it by heart.

For God so loved the world that he gave his one and only Son, that whoever believes in him shall not perish but have eternal life.

Then I ask them to recite 1 John 3:16. Usually only a handful of people are able to do it. Here's what it says:

This is how we know what love is: Jesus Christ laid down his life for us. And we ought to lay down our lives for our brothers.

I point out to audiences that perhaps the reason we memorise John 3:16 is because it tells us Christ gave His life for us. That is something for which we can all give thanks. However, 1 John 3:16 asks us to be willing and ready to give our lives for others. That is not quite as appealing.

In John's Gospel we have recorded the prayer of our Lord before He went to the cross. Francis Schaeffer, commenting on that prayer, said that God has given the world the right to know whether Christianity is real by the way His people relate to one another.

"My prayer is not for them alone. I pray also for those who will believe in me through their message, that all of them may be one, Father, just as you are in me and I am in you. May they also be in us so that the world may believe that you have sent me." (John 17:20–21)

Even the most casual reader of the Scriptures will notice that the Bible fairly bulges with an emphasis on relationships. It has been said that the whole theme of the Bible can be expressed this way: perfect relationships in the Trinity, broken relationships in Eden, restored relationships in Christ.

WHY ARE RELATIONSHIPS SO IMPORTANT?

But why are relationships so important? One of the most important reasons is this: to be is to be in relationships. We come to a sense of our identity, who we are, in a relationship. Clyde Narramore says, "We don't know who we are until we know whose we are."

To be fully human and fully alive we must know something of how to relate. I heard a psychiatrist say on one occasion: "Every maladjusted person is someone who is unable to make himself or herself known to another."

Our maturity as Christians is best seen in the way we relate. I know people who thought they were spiritually mature because they knew their Bibles well. They could quote Scripture and knew the answers to many of the questions put to them about the Bible, but they were not good at relating, and hence they were immature. The core of our maturity as Christians is visible in the way we relate. "Christianity," says one author, "is probably compromised more in our relationships than any other thing."

Through our relationships with other image bearers our characters are moulded. God uses people to help refine people. Non-Christians go to their graves with their character flaws largely unchanged and unaltered, but with you and me it is different.

God wants to make us like Jesus, and one of the ways He goes about doing that is to put us with people who might rub us the wrong way. The finishing touches will be made when we see Christ, but the major shaping of our characters takes place here and now – through our relationships.

Do you realise that the people you work with and relate to are handpicked by the Lord to expose your temper, your pride, your stubbornness – whatever your failings are; and running away from those people is no answer. It's not worth it because God has many more He can manoeuvre into position to replace them. Make a list of all the people you don't get along with and ask yourself, "What is God trying to show me about myself through them?"

Where do we find a better place to put into operation the principles of Scripture than in close relationships? Take marriage for example. How often do we hear of two Christians seeking a divorce because they believe they are incompatible. "Incompatibility," said someone, "is not a reason for divorce. Incompatibility is the reason for marriage."

Opposites attract, and two people in marriage who are opposites in temperament have the opportunity to apply the grace of God to their differences and learn to adjust. There would be far fewer marriage breakups if this was understood and applied.

TRUST IN GOD – THE KEY TO RELATING WELL TO OTHERS

The real problem behind our relationships is the same as that which first disrupted relationships in the Garden of Eden. It has to do with our confidence in the goodness of God. Once the foundation stone of God's goodness is removed from beneath us, we do not have a hope of building good relationships.

The reason for this is that we must have complete trust in God in order to relate to others. Relationships, as I am sure you are aware, sometimes hurt. People, being fallen human beings, can fail. There isn't a person living who hasn't been let down in relationships. In truth, the more we relate to people, the more we are guaranteed to get hurt.

It follows then that we need supernatural support if we are to relate well to others because what often destroys relationships is the fear of getting hurt. When our relationships are governed more by a fear of getting hurt rather than by a desire to love, our relationships will be superficial. We will get close enough to people to be socially acceptable but not close enough to be hurt.

Whenever we are more concerned about our own welfare than we are about the welfare of others, we are not loving as we are loved. There are many definitions of what it means to love. Charles Finney said, "Love is bringing about the highest good in the life of another." A line in *Love Story* defined love as "never having to say you are sorry" – idealistic but hardly realistic.

One of the best definitions of *love* is this: "Love is moving towards others without self-protection." A wonderful example of this type of love is seen in our Lord's encounter with Simon Peter:

When they had finished eating, Jesus said to Simon Peter, "Simon son of John, do you truly love me more than these?" "Yes, Lord," he said, "you know that I love you." Jesus said, "Feed my lambs." Again Jesus said, "Simon son of John, do you truly love me?" He answered, "Yes, Lord, you know that I love you." Jesus said, "Take care of my sheep." The third time he said to him, "Simon son of John, do you love me?" Peter was hurt because Jesus asked him the third time, "Do you love me?" He said, "Lord, you know all things; you know that I love you." Jesus said, "Feed my sheep." (John 21:15–17)

There is no doubt that Simon Peter had a key position in the band of the original disciples. On many occasions he was the spokesman for the group. And he was the one to whom Jesus promised the keys of the kingdom (Matt. 16:19).

Here our Lord asks Simon Peter three times, "Do you truly love me?" That question was calculated to take Peter to the very core of Christianity – a loving relationship with Jesus Christ.

Peter's reply to Christ's first inquiry was, in the words of the NIV, "Yes, you know that I love you." J.B. Phillips, in his translation, says that the word *love* in Jesus' question is the strongest word in the Greek language – *agape*, which means "unconditional love". Peter's reply, however, contained a weaker Greek word, *phileo*, meaning "fondness or friendship". J. B. Phillips translates Peter's reply thus: "You know that I am your friend."

Imagine if you asked someone you loved – a husband, wife, family member, or a fiancée, the question, "Do you love me?" and they replied, "Yes, I am your friend." How do you think you would feel? I asked a woman I was counselling, "If you asked your husband, 'Do you love me?' and he replied, 'I am your friend,' what would you do?" She said, "I would be deeply hurt and certainly would not ask him a second time. And if I knew he really meant it, I would pack my bags and leave."

Was Jesus hurt by Simon Peter's less-than-desirable response? I imagine so. Our Lord was not incapable of being hurt. The writer to the Hebrews tells us He was "touched with the feeling of our infirmities" (Heb. 4:15, AV). The difference between Christ and us is that when we get hurt, we overlay anger on our hurt because anger is a much easier emotion to handle. It gives us a feeling of power. It is a form of self-protection – a device used by the personality to avoid the unpleasantness of hurt.

But in our Lord's heart burned and blazed a love that needed no self-protection. Thus He exposes Himself once more to the possibility of His love's being unreciprocated. So He said to Simon Peter a second time, again using the strong word *agape*, "Simon, son of John, do you love me?" Peter replied, "Yes Lord, you know that I am your friend" (*phileo*).

Our Lord, longing for a positive response from Simon Peter, put the question to him for the third time, but on this occasion He took the word *friend* (*phileo*) off Peter's lips and put it on His own: "Simon, son of John, *are* you my friend?" By using the word Simon Peter had used – *friend* – Christ was saying in effect: "Peter, is that all I mean to you? I know you have been disappointed and that things did not work out as you expected. But I love you nevertheless. Just a little while ago I worked a miracle for you. I gave you 153 fish. If it's fish you want, I can give it to you. But won't you consider what I want? I want your wholehearted love. Won't you give yourself to Me in the way I have given Myself to you?"

Stubborn Peter responded the third time in exactly the same way: "You know I am your friend." Peter failed to come through in the way Christ desired, but Peter's apparent coldness did not freeze the stream of the Saviour's love. He continued to love him, and on the day of Pentecost He fulfilled His promise to Peter by giving him the keys of the kingdom. There through one sermon Simon Peter opened the doors of the Church and three thousand souls came in.

We know that Simon Peter did eventually rise to a much higher level than friendship in his relationship with Jesus Christ. In his two epistles the word *agape* appears several times. Here's just one example:

> *Though you have not seen him, you love [agape] him; and even though you do not see him now, you believe in him and are filled with an inexpressible and glorious joy.* (1 Pet. 1:8)

How could Jesus love so well? What was His secret of being able to move towards others without self-protection? The relationship He had with His Father made Him the most secure man who ever lived. He never had an identity crisis. He knew who He was, why He was here, and also that, though He could not depend on the love of other human beings, He could rest securely in His Father's love – a love that would never be taken away.

Thus, He could move towards others in the knowledge that though they might hurt Him, they could not destroy Him. The strength of His Father's love flowing through Him enabled Him to keep on loving. The love that flowed towards Him on a horizontal level might be tainted with failure but not the love that came down to Him from above. Even when He was devoid of the love and support of His disciples, as He neared the cross He could go on loving just the same.

The apostle Peter brings out this thought most beautifully in chapter 2 of his first epistle:

But if you suffer for doing good and you endure it, this is commendable before God. To this you were called, because Christ suffered for you, leaving you an example, that you should follow in his steps. "He committed no sin, and no deceit was found in his mouth." When they hurled their insults at him, he did not retaliate; when he suffered, he made no threats. Instead, he entrusted himself to him who judges justly. (1 Pet. 2:20–23)

Our Lord was able to respond to all kinds of suffering, insults, scorn, and ridicule because He entrusted Himself to Him who judges justly. This is the only mature response.

In *Parenting Adolescents*, Kevin Huggins says:

A person cannot be free to make another's well being his top priority until he has entrusted his well being to Another. This frees us to relate even in the most painful relationships as Christ did with the goal of being a servant rather than a consumer.

I came across this in my reading of A.W. Tozer a few years ago: "The measure of our relationships with others is the measure of our relationship with God." Scripture expresses that same thought in this way:

If anyone says, "I love God," yet hates his brother, he is a liar. For anyone who does not love his brother, whom he has seen, cannot love God, whom he has not seen. (1 John 4:20)

Relationships are the clearest window through which we can look to see the condition of our souls; relationships can speak to us about how deeply we are trusting God. What is true about our heart's direction with another human being will reveal what our hearts truly feel towards God.

I have noticed that on the human level three styles of relating can be observed. One is moving towards others in order to get something from them. Another is moving away from others in order to avoid them. The third is moving against others to be hostile to them. What is your relational style? Do you relate to God and others on the basis of a trust in Him to look after your deepest welfare so that you are free to direct your energies towards others?

A LOOK IN THE MIRROR

During World War I, a British soldier on the battlefields of France picked up in the ruins of a church a rather nice frame that once contained a picture of Christ. Embossed on the bottom of the frame were the words *Ecco Homo, Behold the Man*. He sent it home as a souvenir, and someone at home put a mirror in the frame and hung it in the entrance hall.

A visitor called at the house soon after, and as he hung up his coat in the entrance hall, looked into the mirror but was startled as he caught sight of the words on the bottom. Knowing what the words meant and that they were taken from Pilate's remark to Jesus, he paused to look and was startled when he saw *himself*.

This is the only place we can truly see ourselves as we are – in Christ. Christ is the mirror of God. We look at Him, and we see God reflected in Him perfectly. He is also the mirror by which we look at ourselves. He reflects a perfect likeness of the image that falls upon Him. We can look into the mirror of Christ and say with truth, "That is the person I am." This revelation for some of us can be appalling, and we can thank God that He saves us from seeing the truth all at once.

So then, let us look at ourselves in Christ. Look into the mirror of that amazing love and then contrast it with yourself. The first thing that strikes any man or woman who does this is an awareness of how much we are taken up with ourselves. It is from this that Christ would deliver us. He wants us to crucify that arrogant, dominating self and having crucified it, replace it with His own unselfishness. Do you have faith for this to happen? Draw close to Him and He will draw close to you. Open your whole being to Him, and He will open His whole being to you. And never forget that the life of God comes fully into us as it is allowed to go freely through us.

> Freely to all ourselves we give
> Constrained by Jesu's love to live,
> The servants of mankind.

A SPIRITUAL CHECKUP

One of the steps to growing and maturing spiritually is to get to know yourself. Take some time to understand the forces within you that cause you problems, forces like James describes in 4:1–3.

Take this test at least once a month or whenever you feel yourself off track spiritually.

1. Am I treating my physical body with the respect and consideration that ought to characterise a tenant of God's property? (Poor physical functioning may sometimes be the cause of a low spiritual condition.)

2. Are my deep longings for security, self-worth and significance being met in my relationship with God, or am I still hankering for them to be met through more visible things – earthly relationships, career, possessions or accomplishments?

3. How effective am I at countering the foolish idea that life can be found by acting independently of God?

4. When strong and incapacitating emotions surge within me – such as anger, anxiety and guilt – can I trace them to an obstacle that may be interfering with a chosen goal?

5. How aware am I that I am a choosing being? Do I blame others or circumstances for my feelings of distress?

6. In setting goals for myself, am I governed by the same controlling desire of the apostle Paul to please him? Read 2 Corinthians 5:9.

7. Do I know how to bring my thoughts under control?

8. Do I understand the importance of repentance? Am I clear on the differences between remorse, regret, reformation and reparation?

9. Am I aware that my goals depend on what I believe will meet my needs? Have I truly grasped this intellectually and spiritually?

10. What steps am I taking to think biblically about issues? Is my mind oriented to Scripture? How much time do I spend with God in prayer and in the Bible?

11. Does self-interest rule my life? How much of my life is given to the needs of others?

12. How much am I growing?*

*Those who respond negatively to this question should not allow the situation to remain as it is. Seek the help of your pastor or a Christian counsellor. And always remember, although God longs for you to grow in grace and in knowledge of Him that is not a condition for His loving you. Divine love is constant, no matter what.

ACKNOWLEDGEMENTS

The list of factors motivating human behaviour on pages 18 and 19 are based on a list of counselling theories by David Powlinson, in *Journal of Biblical Counseling* 18 (autumn, 1999): p.1.

The list of why it is important to know who God is was prompted by Charles Swindoll's *Growing Deep in the Christian Life* (Grand Rapids: Zondervan, 1995), p.93.

Beginning on page 139, I discuss identity using the alliterative words *security, self-worth* and *significance*. Larry Crabb uses these three words in a way different from the way I use them. He sees security and significance as being the routes down which we go to experience self-worth. I see them as three distinct entities. For more on Dr Crabb's views regarding these three words, see his *Biblical Principles of Effective Counseling* (Grand Rapids: Zondervan, 1975). Dr Crabb's book *Understanding People* (London: Marshall Pickering, 1998) is the foundation for my thinking in Chapters 8 and 9.

NATIONAL DISTRIBUTERS

UK: (and countries not listed below)
CWR, Waverley Abbey House, Waverley Lane, Farnham, Surrey GU9 8EP.
Tel: (01252) 784710 Outside UK (44) 1252 784710

AUSTRALIA: CMC Australasia, PO Box 519, Belmont, Victoria 3216.
Tel: (03) 5241 3288

CANADA: CMC Distribution Ltd, PO Box 7000, Niagara on the Lake, Ontario L0S 1JO.
Tel: 1800 325 1297

GHANA: Challenge Enterprises of Ghana, PO Box 5723, Accra.
Tel: (021) 222437/223249 Fax: (021) 226227

HONG KONG: Cross Communications Ltd, 1/F, 562A Nathan Road, Kowloon.
Tel: 2780 1188 Fax: 2770 6229

INDIA: Crystal Communications, 10-3-18/4/1, East Marredpally, Secunderabad – 500 026.
Tel/Fax: (040) 7732801

KENYA: Keswick Bookshop, PO Box 10242, Nairobi.
Tel: (02) 331692/226047 Fax: (02) 728557

MALAYSIA: Salvation Book Centre (M) Sdn Bhd, 23 Jalan SS 2/64, 47300 Petaling Jaya,
Selangor. Tel: (03) 78766411/78766797 Fax: (03) 78757066/78756360

NEW ZEALAND: CMC Australasia, PO Box 36015, Lower Hutt.
Tel: 0800 449 408 Fax: 0800 449 049

NIGERIA: FBFM, Helen Baugh House, 96 St Finbarr's College Road, Akoka, Lagos.
Tel: (01) 7747429/4700218/825775/827264

PHILIPPINES: OMF Literature Inc, 776 Boni Avenue, Mandaluyong City.
Tel: (02) 531 2183 Fax: (02) 531 1960

REPUBLIC OF IRELAND: Scripture Union, 40 Talbot Street, Dublin 1.
Tel: (01) 8363764

SINGAPORE: Campus Crusade Asia Ltd, 315 Outram Road, 06-08 Tan Boon Liat Building,
Singapore 169074. Tel: 222 3640

SOUTH AFRICA: Struik Christian Books, 80 MacKenzie Street, PO Box 1144, Cape Town
8000. Tel: (021) 462 4360 Fax: (021) 461 3612

SRI LANKA: Christombu Books, 27 Hospital Street, Colombo 1.
Tel: (01) 433142/328909

TANZANIA: CLC Christian Book Centre, PO Box 1384, Mkwepu Street, Dar es Salaam.
Tel/Fax (022) 2119439

USA: CMC Distribution, PO Box 644, Lewiston, New York, 14092-0644.
Tel: 1800 325 1297

ZIMBABWE: Word of Life Books, Shop 4, Memorial Building, 35 S Machel Avenue, Harare.
Tel: (04) 781305 Fax: (04) 774739

For e-mail addresses, visit the CWR web site: www.cwr.org.uk